the PERFECTLY IMPERFECT CHURCH

REDEFINING the "IDEAL" CHURCH

STEVE SJOGREN

the PERFECTLY IMPERFECT CHURCH

REDEFINING the "IDEAL" CHURCH

Flagship church resources
from Group Publishing

the PERFECTLY IMPERFECT CHURCH

REDEFINING the "IDEAL" CHURCH

Visit our Web site: **www.grouppublishing.com**

CREDITS
Author: *Steve Sjogren*
Creative Development Editor: *Paul Woods*
Chief Creative Officer: *Joani Schultz*
Assistant Editor: *Alison Imbriaco*
Book Designer: *Jean Bruns*
Computer Graphic Artist: *Joyce Douglas*
Cover Art Director: *Jeff A. Storm*
Cover Designer: *Blukazoo Studio*
Illustrator: *Matt Wood*
Production Manager: *Peggy Naylor*

LIBRARY OF CONGRESS CATALOGING-IN-PUBLICATION DATA
Sjogren, Steve, 1955-
The perfectly imperfect church : redefining the "ideal" church / by Steve Sjogren.
p. cm.
Includes bibliographical references.
ISBN 0-7644-2353-3 (pbk. : alk. paper)
1. Church I. Title.
BV600.3 .S57 2002
250--dc21 2002003973
10 9 8 7 6 5 4 3 2 1 11 10 09 08 07 06 05 04 03 02

Printed in the United States of America.

Contents

Section A
The Aha! Experience

Section B
Paths to the Perfectly Imperfect Church

Foreword

This book is designed to encourage the leaders of two kinds of churches.

I have written this book primarily to church leaders who are struggling with survival issues. I hope the following pages will help church leaders who have fewer than two hundred in regular weekend attendance grow to the point of becoming a Perfectly Imperfect Church, with a weekend attendance of three to five hundred. To you my message is, "You can do it!" What is laid out in this book is attainable by the average small church.

This book is also written to encourage church leaders who are building Launching-Pad Churches, with a weekend attendance of one thousand or more. You are overgrown Perfectly Imperfect Churches! The same skill set will help the larger version grow.

It doesn't take a spectacular and unusual church to build the kind of group that can make a difference. It isn't beyond your grasp to put together an organization that can really have an impact on your city.

It doesn't take a church-growth genius to grow the kind of church that is described in these pages, because we aren't talking about the rare leader who comes along every once in a while. We are talking about your church leaders and about the gifts that are already present in your leaders and in your already-gathered people.

Steve Sjogren
Cincinnati, Ohio

Acknowledgements

Thanks for the deep thoughts from my deep friends: Dave Workman, Dana Cochran, Jim Cochran, Rob Lewin (I can type almost as fast as you talk), Steve Bowen, Robert Pittman, and Todd Hunter.

Dedication

To Doug Hanto.
Thanks for giving me a second chance at life.
You're more than a "pretty good" doctor!

Section A

The Aha! Experience

The Aha! Experience

Sometimes I see things for the first time after a thousand glances.

As a friendly consultant, I had walked into First Community Church so often that I quit keeping track of my time. The leadership told me repeatedly that their goal was to "become something great for God." But after being with them for more than a hundred hours, I concluded that they were aspiring to a level of imagined greatness that they were not destined for in reality.

The pastor was a good guy, but not off-the-charts gifted. He could deliver a message well enough, but I suspected that he would never become well-known as an author or speaker. I was fairly certain I would not be seeing him on Christian TV. The church was doing outreach programs in the community that were competent. The people genuinely loved one another—that was clear. Their worship times were genuine. When I was with them, even though I didn't know all the songs, I could feel the presence of the Lord.

People felt a sense of safety, at multiple levels, at their services, and that feeling of safety allowed them to bring their friends to services. Safety was one of the leading causes for their numerical growth. Fun people to be with, they embraced newcomers quickly. Love and trust abounded in their small groups.

People seemed to understand intuitively what it takes for a church to grow, so the atmosphere they created fostered growth. Generosity marked the way these folks related to people outside their ranks. Having long ago given up arguing over small doctrinal issues, their motto was, "Focus on the main and the plain." One of their greatest joys was to promote other churches in the city in various ways. And they promoted leaders from within, feeling it was best for the church.

Thinking about all these factors, I had what Norwegians call an *Aha opplevelse* (UP-level-suh), which can be roughly translated as an "Aha! experience" although it means much more. It means seeing something with new eyes. It means jump up and down and get so excited you start to march around the room in virtually unbridled enthusiasm shouting,

"WOW! Now I get it! It all makes sense now."

Aha! 1:
Imperfect can be perfect.

First Community Church wasn't called to be spectacular by the narrow definition that's been drummed into my head by an untold number of books, articles, and word-of-mouth myths. The people in its congregation weren't called to be anything but themselves.

I had it in my head that there was one sort of church to be if one really wanted to count in the world of churches. I thought a church that counted had to be in the top 1 percent of churches—a church with at least one thousand people. But First Community Church was doing well in virtually every measurable respect. After years of being together, the congregation managed to pull together about four hundred people each Sunday—no small feat, all things considered.

My Aha! moment brought the realization that this church was doing excellent things for the cause of Christ at its current size. The church wasn't perfect, but it was pretty good! It was a Perfectly Imperfect Church.

OTHER FALSE ASSUMPTIONS

We make a mistake when we evaluate a church's success strictly in terms of numerical growth or technique. Alan Roxburgh described this misplaced emphasis in *Missionary Congregation, Leadership & Liminality:*

"Numerical growth is the talisman of our ecclesiological health... Technique is the primary method for reestablishing the church's place in the culture. God is but a legitimating footnote of ecclesiology...

The Harvard School of Business, Faith Popcorn, and George Barna are the contemporary saints." [1]

Aha! 2:
Bigger is not better, nor is it more effective.

Not so long ago, the so-called megachurches were all the rage. During the '80s and '90s, How can I grow a giant-sized church? was the burning question in church leadership circles. Thankfully the megachurch trend is fading.

We've seen churches grow large in record numbers during the past twenty years, but history has shown that church health does not come hand in hand with that numerical growth. The burning issue for the next few decades, it seems, will be church health.

In spite of a few highly visible ones, the megachurch is a dinosaur. As numbers pass the one-thousand mark, church health is increasingly difficult to maintain.

Aha! 3:
Church health is measured by competence, not competition.

How can you know whether or not you're doing what you should?

Scan through the pages of Charisma, Ministries Today, or most issues of Christianity Today, and you will find a bipolar message. Mixed in with the help the magazines offer are lots of subliminal messages, including:

- If your church counts, it will be large—very large, in fact.
- If you count as a leader, you will look like, talk like, teach like, and lead like the guys who are getting national attention. (Very white teeth, a big smile, a striking Italian suit—you've seen the pictures or have been to the conferences.)
- If you hope to go anywhere with your church, you had better get yourself to the "happening" conferences where you can learn to emulate these magicians.

The underlying message seems to be that the more you're like the pastors of large churches, the more confident you can be that you're doing what you should. However, imitating leaders of large churches—striving to have the most welcoming smile, the most inspiring speeches, and, of course, the biggest numbers—can cause pastors to become competitive.

Action is a good thing, but overly stimulated and undirected action can become destructive. It can resemble an overdose of caffeine. Don't get me wrong; I've been a coffee drinker for years. I enjoy the smell, the taste, the entire experience of coffee. However, I learned recently that it is possible to drink a lethal dose of java (suicide by Starbucks?). The thought is staggering. If a person who weighs about 150 pounds consumes some eighty cups of drip coffee in a short time, some really bad things will happen to his or her heart, kidneys, and liver. [2]

We don't need an outside stimulant to do the work of the Spirit. He is ready, willing, and able to fill us with his power to change the world. (I wonder if some of the leaders of the megachurches who have been presented to us as models are on major doses of caffeine.)

I've walked away de-energized from leadership conferences that were supposed to be encouraging and uplifting. Typically, I spend the first day of the conference listening to the pastor of a gigantic church who is trying really hard to convince me that he's just like me. He then goes into his approach to church life, an approach that has spawned his many books on the topic. By the second day, I'm not feeling so good about the conference, myself—or my ministry, for that matter. Then it hits me: I'm not listening to a regular person. This is superman! No wonder I'm discouraged. I can't compete. I could never compete. There is little if anything this person does that intersects with my life because he is just that extraordinary.

While conferences and publications offer helpful advice, unintended messages can damage the souls of their followers. These subtle messages can lead to the conclusion that we are involved in a competition to outdo one another to become bigger, faster, more, and better by growing a BIG church.

In this book, I'm describing what I call the Perfectly Imperfect Church, because a church doesn't have to fit the reigning definition of perfect to have a powerful ministry. I tend to interchange the term *Perfectly Imperfect Church* with the *Pretty Good Church.* This second term stems from psychologist Abraham Maslow's hierarchy of human needs. He observed that we all have basic needs for survival. These are physical needs for food, water, and shelter. Once those basic needs are met, we have more advanced social needs, such as the need to belong. People exist at all levels of the hierarchy.

At the top of the pyramid of needs are the few hearty souls Maslow calls self-actualized. With all their needs being met, they no longer crave affirmation. Instead they give it away to others. In Maslow's model, the parents who qualify as the best parents are what he called good enough parents. They aren't the pushy, aggressive ones who seek to live out their lives vicariously through their children by constantly intruding. Good enough parents aren't the ones you see at their kids' soccer games, yelling at the refs for making a questionable call. They're not the ones scolding their children for not winning the game. They don't scold a child for getting a B+ instead of an A-. Good enough parents are great listeners and affirmers who seek to help their children become successful in whatever field of interest their children have in their hearts to pursue. Good enough parents are not competitive; they are affirming in the journey of life.

Today's overemphasis on the pursuit of excellence has led to a highly competitive attitude among churches and church leaders that's not matched in recent history. Dr. Maslow wouldn't have been surprised. He found that overaggressive behavior indicates a person who has not progressed very far in the journey of life. I interpret that to mean that the goal shouldn't be to be better than the church down the street or to build a church larger than the one across town. Those uninspired ideas likely come out of someone's lack of a healthy self-image. The church world beckons to us to do more, better, faster than the guys down the street. But we don't have to fall into that trap. We don't have to be perfect. We're OK being a Pretty Good Church!

Aha! 4: *The best churches may not be the most visible ones.*

There exists an unofficial "CPC" (church politically correct) thought in the church world. I don't want to sound like a conspiracy theorist, but perhaps there's even an agenda in the popular Christian media to promote certain groups, congregations, and individual heroes—to lionize them while ignoring others who are doing a great job.

The churches being presented as super-successful are virtually impossible to gain any encouragement from because they are so distinctive. In spite of their good intent, many of the leadership conferences sponsored by these megachurches tend to be discouraging. After seeing the perfect execution of the apparently flawless church, conference attendees leave thinking, "Hey, we'll never get there. We'll never raise that much money. We'll never recruit that many gifted leaders. Our people will never respond like these people. This will never work at our place."

The best churches in America vary significantly. They are sometimes large. They are sometimes small. Often they are medium-sized (with weekend attendance of three to five hundred). They are usually not easy to explain, and their nonconformance with accepted practices may even seem iconoclastic. The Christian media isn't entirely comfortable with the leadership of these churches, because many of the leaders aren't exactly like "us." T.D. Jakes, who shot out of nowhere to national prominence, is an interesting example. The multi-ethnic church he founded in Dallas in 1996, The Potter's House, suddenly has over twenty-six thousand members. [3] The popular Christian media doesn't know what to do with Jakes. I've heard people ask, "Who is the next Billy Graham?" I wonder if it isn't Jakes. Like Graham, he came into sudden national prominence in spite of having few resources. His success is virtually impossible to explain without a large God element.

Four Kinds of Churches

Based on the significance of these Aha! experiences, I've identified four kinds of churches. As you'll see, they vary in health and effectiveness.

THE STRUGGLING CHURCH

Typical of the vast majority of churches in America is the church with a weekend attendance of fewer than two hundred that's just trying to keep on keeping on. Like it or not, it takes two hundred people to support a church. Because of all it takes to maintain the cultural expectation of what a church should be, two hundred regular attendees, adults and children, is the break-even point in America. A church is not truly viable until it hits that two-hundred mark.

Calling a church struggling because of its size is no doubt offensive to some. I don't mean to be disrespectful of the struggling church. I've been the leader of three of them for an extended time. But these churches really are struggling in many senses. They are not large enough to do the things that our culture associates with church: quality worship, child care, teen ministry, and an active lay leadership, to name a few.

A recent poll conducted by Barna Research found that 40 percent of the 3764 Protestant churches contacted had no one answering the phone. On top of that, half of those churches (44 percent) didn't even have an answering machine, something that would go a long way toward saying to the public, "We're interested in your call." [4] These statistics tell a lot about the struggle to keep the fires going.

Being a veteran leader of struggling churches, I know about the emotional and spiritual stress that is present in these organizations. Every day is a struggle.

- The goal is to survive from week to week.
- Constant effort is required just to keep things afloat.
- One family leaving creates a crisis.
- Leading is not fun.
- Involvement for a prolonged period is unhealthy at every level for everyone involved.

Being in a struggling church is much like being a part of a sailboat crew that isn't quite large enough to make a safe open-water journey. It's scary and unpleasant for all.

My friend Tim Smith helped sail an eighty-foot yacht on a twelve-hundred-mile journey from the Virgin Islands to North Carolina. Just before the yacht sailed, the crew of ten was reduced to just five. However, the captain was a bit overly enthusiastic, and he was armed with a good weather report. They set sail.

At first, the trip was absolute bliss. Tim saw a seagull riding on the back of a sea turtle at high sea. Whales came right up to the side of the yacht. It was magical. But it wasn't long before the five absent crew members were sorely missed.

Reports of fair weather had been less than accurate. Storms moved in, and sea swells kicked up. Soon the crew encountered the Gulf Stream current, which flows north, as they sought to head west. Within a couple of days, they went from balmy, idyllic seas to a full-fledged, batten-down-the-hatches storm.

The crew was stretched to the max in good weather; when bad weather hit, they were overwhelmed. They were no longer having fun. My friend Tim wondered openly if he was ever going to see his wife and children again. The yacht's crew finally did make port, but with a few more gray hairs and a firm determination to never board an undermanned boat again.

Struggling churches may seem fun at first, even a little adventurous. An element of excitement comes with starting something new and striking out in a pioneering work. But the struggles stop being fun after a rather short time. And none of us do anything that isn't enjoyable for long. After a while, struggling churches can become toxic to all involved. We actually become emotionally sick from a church situation that drains us, with no end in sight.

The goal of this book is to empower the leaders of struggling churches with the skills they need to become leaders of Pretty Good Churches. Not perfect, but Perfectly Imperfect!

THE EGO-DRIVEN CHURCH

This church is the worst of the megachurch world. Have you ever driven into a town and seen a billboard advertising a church—and most of the billboard is a photo of the pastor's face? Or have you been around a church that is large—even super-large—yet refuses to multiply through local church planting? Or have you been around a church that keeps adding on to its facility for no apparent reason? If so, perhaps you've been around the second sort of unhealthy church structure, the ego-driven church.

- It has no great or redemptive reason for the desire to be large; it just wants to be large!

- It has over one thousand in weekend attendance (or acts as if it's very large).
- It is senior-pastor-centered.
- It is fearful of launching new churches.
- It lacks clear identity (the focus changes every two to four years).

Such a church is an inwardly focused place. While there might be talk of outreach, there is actually little or no real outreach going on. Just as bad is the medium-sized church trying to appear larger than it is. The problem with both is that they don't know why they are trying to be large; they just really like being L-A-R-G-E!

A megachurch can be a healthy church if it is willing to give itself away. However, I honestly have never seen an ego-driven church make the switch to a healthy place.

I know of a number of well-known megachurches that, unfortunately, absolutely refuse to plant other churches. In fact, some are going to extremes to not expand by multiplication. They are raising tremendous amounts of money to build amazing facilities that will allow upward of ten thousand people to assemble at one time. My question is, What are those churches going to do when the magical, mystical senior leader passes from the scene? In each case, the popularity of the pastor is what keeps the system going forward.

THE LAUNCHING-PAD CHURCH

The first sort of healthy structure is the Launching-Pad Church. This is the best of what the megachurch has to offer. It regularly uses its largesse to spawn new congregations.

- It has a regular attendance of more than one thousand.
- It is ordained by God.
- It is financed by God.
- It has a deep bench depth (talent pool).
- It consistently sees birthing new congregations as normal and reproduces itself in a variety of ways.

The prominent churches in the New Testament were all Launching-Pad Churches. Today's Launching-Pad Churches are "teaching churches," offering internships throughout the structure. Staff members not only do their jobs but also oversee outsiders who are peering over their shoulders to learn how effective ministry is done. These are "laboratory churches" that continually try new approaches to learning and ministry.

You can't just go away for the weekend with the local church leadership and decide you're going to build yourself a Launching-Pad Church. It is up to God. God needs to call your church to be one of these. It takes sovereign amounts of money, sovereign amounts of talent, sovereign amounts of vision—all of which need to be supplied by God regularly.

> *"There is always an enormous temptation in all of life to diddle around making itsy-bitsy friends and meals and journeys for itsy-bitsy years on end. It is so self-conscious, so apparently moral…I won't have it." We are raising tomatoes when we should be raising Cain, or Lazarus."* [5]
>
> —Annie Dillard

THE PRETTY GOOD CHURCH

There is a second church structure that is healthy, and it is the focus of this book. Like Goldilocks finding the "just right" porridge, it's the church of three to five hundred that's "just right" in most settings. The summary glance at this church shows:

- It has an average total weekend attendance of three to five hundred.
- It is competence, not competition, oriented. It's the "good enough" church.
- It is large enough to be able to plant a new church now and then.
- It is large enough to be able to enjoy the strength of a varied staff.

During the last couple of decades, everything in the church has been subject to comparisons. For a pastor, the question begins, "Are you like...?" and concludes by naming the leader of a well-known church that has great visibility somewhere in the world. We've been steeped in the disciple-making church, the seeker-targeted church, the prophetic church, the power-of-the-Spirit church, and the gifts-of-the-Spirit church. We were drowning in a sea of hyphens! The above list only names the hyphenated approaches I've tried over the past decade and a half. I'm embarrassed about the shenanigans I've led my people through. There's no end to tangents. No doubt these will come upon the church until the return of Christ.

I have a simple thought. Maybe it's too simple, but here it is. What if we gave up trying to be any of the specialized churches from this point forward. I have already given up. From now on I refuse to put a hyphen in my descriptive name. I will no longer describe myself as a seeker-sensitive or purpose-driven church.

All of the well-known examples of these specialized churches can offer good testimonies. At the same time, none can be reproduced with any semblance of the success of the original because the key, it turns out (big surprise), is the founder of the concept: the one-of-a-kind apostolic leader. I've read all the books by these one-of-a-kind leaders, and not one acknowledges this fact.

I'm not looking for another fill-in-the blank, hyphenated church. Those journeys are for souls younger, less traveled, and more enthusiastic than mine. If anything, I seek the generic church.

The older I get, the simpler I like things. I wonder, what if we adopted the simplest definitions Jesus gave us for the purpose of life? Jesus said to love God with all our hearts and souls and then to love our neighbors as ourselves. In Jesus' words, we find a picture of a church operating at a practical level, without an agenda or program. We see a church that lives out the truths that it is better to give than to receive and better to love than to be loved.

I dream of a simple church that is marked by the simple proposition that we are otherly.

I have spent about twenty years operating on my belief that the only good and relevant church was the big church with a weekend attendance of more than one thousand—the kind of church that is among the largest in its city and on the road to becoming nationally known. When I came to Cincinnati, I set out to plant that sort of church. Deep in my heart, I felt that if my church and the churches I started didn't grow to that size they weren't really accomplishing what God sent us out to accomplish.

Over the past few years I've begun to seriously rethink that assumption. I've come to believe that, instead of having one church with a weekend attendance of six thousand, which is the size of the Cincinnati church I started, I would much rather have twelve five-hundred-size churches spread throughout the city. Or maybe even twenty churches with three hundred attending each. This awakening has utterly altered my perspective.

Some have asked, "When you use the terms *Pretty Good Church* or *Perfectly Imperfect Church*, aren't you contradicting Scripture that talks about Paul's vision of the church without spot or wrinkle?"

Let me make this clear: I am not making a theological statement with the term *Pretty Good*. Rather I am contrasting Pretty Good with what I see as the predominating spirit of this church age, which is marked by a penchant for extremes in excellence. The modern evangelical church—the seeker-sensitive church—seems to have come to the conclusion that, if we are to do it, we need to do more than do it just right—we need to do it with great excellence. I like the words of Christian thinker and writer G.K. Chesterton who said, "Anything worth doing is worth doing wrong." When he spoke those words one hundred years ago, he prophetically saw that we would struggle in our day, that we would be tempted to fall down at the feet of excellence and worship it instead of using it as a simple tool for ministry.

As we proceed through this book, we're going to begin with simplicity, and then focus on a total of thirteen paths that will lead us to an understanding of the Perfectly Imperfect Church.

1. Simple
2. Upward
3. Outward
4. Anointed
5. Fun
6. Safe
7. Inclusive
8. Trusting
9. Atmospheric
10. Generous
11. True

12. Cooperative
13. Leading Out

Let's launch out from here and look in detail at each of these paths on our journey toward making our churches what God wants them to be.

ENDNOTES

1. Alan J. Roxburgh, *The Missionary Congregation, Leadership, and Liminality* (Harrisburg, PA: Trinity Press, 1979) 20.
2. Bennett Alan Weinberg and Bonnie K. Bealer, *The World of Caffeine* (New York: Routledge, 2001), 313.
3. see www.thepotterhouseinternational.com
4. "Telephoning Churches Often Proves Fruitless," Barna Research Online (August 22, 2000).
5. Annie Dillard, *Three by Annie Dillard* (New York: HarperCollins Publishers, 1990), 258.

Paths to the Perfectly Imperfect Church

Paths to the Perfectly Imperfect Church

Path 1: SIMPLE

A friend of mine was preaching in Kenya a couple of years ago. Part of his purpose was to convey the essence of servant evangelism: that as you serve people with the kindness and generosity of Christ, they open up to the gospel. In one church of several hundred people, everyone became excited about showing God's love in practical ways. In fact, the people became downright stoked!

One Sunday the pastor announced spontaneously that all were invited to gather the next Saturday morning at the church and go out to do a project together. To everyone's surprise, nearly everyone in the church showed up! Armed with containers, the people locked arms to form a human daisy chain and went out into the community to pick up every speck of trash they could find. The pastor described them as a human vacuum cleaner. As they made their way through the city, you could actually see where the kingdom of light had come and where it had not yet come!

The cleanup stunned people around town that day. Everyone the people from that church came in contact with asked about what they were doing. One of the curious was a writer for Kenya's national newspaper. She asked lots of questions along the lines of "Why in the world are you doing this?" When people responded that they were doing just what Jesus would be doing if he were in Eldoret, Kenya, the writer said, "I always thought this is the sort of thing that Jesus would be doing if he came to town."

The writer was sufficiently impressed to write a great story about the outreach, include a photo of the church people, and place it on the front page of the weekend edition of the nationwide paper.

The beauty of that story isn't that people did something great in the kingdom of God and were recognized for it; in picking up trash, they did something very basic. What's significant is that they got excited about serving, they went out and did a simple thing, and they affected their community immediately.

That's beautiful simplicity.

I wonder how many American congregations would respond similarly. How many congregations would get that excited about doing something so practical? How many pastors would have the desire (or authority) to stand up and say, "Let's go for it this Saturday"? I suspect in many cases a number of meetings would need to take place before something like this could happen. And when it finally did happen, it wouldn't be announced to the entire church; that would be too forward. A select few would be invited, and far fewer would attend.

> ***Jesus was the simplest—***
> ***and most effective—person ever.***

Jesus' purpose in life came down to one sentence: "By myself I can do nothing...I seek not to please myself but him who sent me" (John 5:30). That was his guiding philosophy in life and the way he approached all of ministry. He uttered these words immediately after healing a man who had been lame all his life. This man was just one of many in the crowd of perhaps a hundred or more. Jesus walked through the crowd, likely stepping past many who may have been equally disabled or ill, and went directly to just that one man. Jesus offered healing to that one man only. After seeing that solitary person healed, everyone was amazed, including the apostles. They were trying to make sense of this experience. Why had just one been healed? Weren't others worthy of healing? Why did this healing experience seem so fickle? The Pharisees were also upset—even though they had just seen Jesus heal a man lame from birth—because Jesus said he was equal with God.

Jesus didn't address any of the issues that were on people's minds. Instead he made this a matter of the heart. He put it all back to his relationship with the Father: "I judge only as I hear, and my judgement is just, for I seek not to please myself but him who sent me" (John 5:30).

The Hard Way of Simplicity

When Jesus called people to repent and believe in him, he used a phrase that, according to *The Challenge of Jesus* by N.T. Wright, was the dynamic equivalent of a modern command to "give up your own agenda and trust in me." [1] Jesus calls us through that original band of believers to an agenda of simplicity. To pull that off, we must trust him deeply.

Simple and effective. Those two words ought to go together in the church.

Consider the simply effective lives of these people:

Have you read about the guy they call What's Your Name? He's a man who sports long hair and a beard, dresses like one of the apostles, and is wandering the country doing small acts of kindness in the name of Christ. He owns nothing beyond what he wears. When people ask his name, he answers, "What's your name?"

"But has he been effective in his task?" you ask. People have reported physical healings (one man said that What's Your Name laid his hands on the man's ailing car and it started!). In Hazleton, Pennsylvania, his ministry to the teens caused many to give God a chance. He has prayed for people in the hospital who have been healed and released from their symptoms. Local clergy report that hundreds have returned to church as a direct result of the ministry of What's Your Name. If that's not simple effectiveness, it will do until the real thing comes along! [2]

Another example of simple effectiveness is George Smith, head janitor for a suburban St. Louis high school. Just hours after buffing the gymnasium floor at Fern Ridge High School, he was standing on it in cap and gown. The thirty-two seniors of the graduating class chose George Smith as their commencement speaker. The seniors said they chose him, not because of the job he does, but because of the man he is. One graduate said: "He's been so much more than just a janitor. He's helped, you know? He'll talk to you if you have a problem...And he's just a wonderful person."

The national news caught wind of George's story and asked him, "What's the largest group of people you'd spoken to before this?"

His response: "I guess about four or five guys at a backyard barbecue or something."

"This is the greatest honor that I have received," Smith said. "And now, even at my favorite gas station...people are pointing and saying, 'Hey, that's the guy we seen on TV,' you know? So it's changed my life." [3]

Kim Corbin is the head of a worldwide movement of skippers. It's not a fellowship of sea captains; skippers are people who skip wherever they go. They have discovered the joy and the many health benefits associated with the childhood practice of skipping. [4] Life can be defined in the simplest terms of success and failure when the parameters come down to "Are you skipping everywhere you go, or are you not skipping?" The skippers know that they are fulfilling their mission in life if they are skipping everywhere they go. If they merely walk or run or—heaven forbid—ride a bike, they are skipocrits!

Have you heard of the SoulSurvivor movement in the UK? In a country that isn't exactly known for its vibrant churches, this group gathers a couple of times a year to do just two things: worship and serve. By day they hit the streets in a variety of ways. They are especially fond of sprucing up dilapidated sections of town that need a good cleaning or a fresh coat of paint. Serving all day gives them an appetite for worship. They gather each evening for several hours of encountering God through intense and intimate worship.

Simple Discovery: *Dechurched people want simplicity.*

The "dechurched" are those people who have given up on organized religion because it's too complicated, too irrelevant, and not worth the time and effort of getting involved. What they are looking for is what is understandable, simple, and straightforward in the language of the common person.

The dechurched are far more difficult to reach and communicate with than the merely "unchurched" of the '80s and '90s. They are looking for authenticity, transparency, and reality. They won't have it any other way. If you ask a dechurched person why he doesn't attend, he will likely tell you, "It's just not worth it. It takes too much energy to get to a place that is too out of touch with life. Once I get there, I'm not edified. In fact, I'm bummed out. Then once I leave, it takes a couple of days to recover emotionally. Frankly, I have better things to do with my life."

Many of the dechurched are believers. They love the Lord; they just can't handle the complexity of the church as it has come to be.

Of those who don't attend church, only 2 percent stay away because they don't believe in God. The rest simply can't handle church for one reason or another.[5] Actually they can't handle church for a lot of reasons. For those who have ears to hear, the message is clear: People are looking for something more simple and straightforward.

Simple Discovery: *Definition is essential for success.*

I used to do a fair bit of target shooting with some friends of mine at an indoor target range. I invested quite a bit of money in my equipment and became pretty accurate. I became extremely accurate when I purchased a laser sight for one of my pistols. Once the pistol was "sighted in," hitting the center of the target was hardly a sport . The bull's-eye, even at the end of the range, was easy to hit every time, as long as the gun was steadied.

Every so often that same indoor range has what's called Machine Gun Night. Machine gun owners in the area are invited to come out and shoot for free for the evening. The best part, for a target shooter, is that anyone who wants to shoot can also have a go at firing a real, live machine gun as long as he or she provides the ammunition.

The first time I fired a machine gun, I was completely unprepared for the experience. I had seen plenty of movies where the hero comes along and saves the day with machine guns blazing in both hands at the same time. In reality, they are just about impossible to keep steady. They are incredibly inaccurate and tend to move upward as they are fired. In my ignorance, I ended up blasting away at the ceiling!

The way most leaders in the church approach leadership is more like wildly firing a machine gun than carefully aiming a laser-sighted weapon. Most churches don't know who they are, why they exist, or where they are headed, and they don't have the foggiest idea how they are going to get there. "Who are we? Who aren't we? Where are we going?" are all mystifying questions in many churches.

It is essential that we clarify our reason for being and our vision. If we hope to be effective, we must communicate these guiding factors and get the powers that be on board at the same time.

The words *church* and *complication* are too often synonymous. In my travels around the country, I am finding that new church plants are commonly being advised that, unless they have several hundred thousand dollars in hand, they dare not start their work. Too many leaders are frozen in their tracks, not knowing where to go in the current maze of complication the church finds itself in.

The church is drowning in a sea of complication.

We need to take heed of Ockham's razor, a principle put forward by the medieval monk William Ockham. Also known as the law of economy, this rule states that we should not increase, beyond what is necessary, the number of entities required to explain anything. The greater the complexity of the system, the greater the need for simplicity. We need to get rid of the extraneous and get back to basics. The most complex things humans have created come from the most plenteous and simple things found in nature: sand, oxygen, water, fire.

Jesus had a reason for doing everything he did. He lived on purpose.

Simple Discovery: *The straightforward approach to services is the best approach.*

THE SIXTY-MINUTE SERVICE

Over the years, I have experimented with service lengths that varied from less than an hour to two hours. I have come to the conclusion that sixty minutes is just right. There's something special about an hour. Something about that sixty-minute period seems to be hard-wired into the human psyche. LensCrafters optical stores have made a lot of money because they promise to take care of people "in about an hour." The reality in our culture dictates that people can't endure more than one hour.

Not many churches really do an hour-long service. We try to cram too much in. Some of us may feel that by limiting services to an hour we're accommodating the culture too much. Tension will always exist between what is culturally relevant and what is biblically counter-culture.

Following are the service elements I see as most effective.

THE WELCOME

At Vineyard Community Church, we start by telling people what we're going to do while we're together. We say, "We're glad you've chosen to invest the next hour with us. Here's what we'll be doing. We'll sing a few songs with catchy choruses that are easy to learn. The words will be on the screen at the front if you aren't familiar with them. Then someone is going to tell you what's going on around here this week. Then we'll look at a video [or see a drama or hear from someone for a minute]. Finally, someone is going to talk from the Bible in a very practical way for twenty-five to thirty minutes. This will be the fastest hour of your week."

When we tell people what we're going to do, they can relax because they know exactly what's going to happen. What we do is much like what a host does at a fine restaurant. He or she makes people feel at home by telling them what to expect and what the specials of the house are.

> ***PowerPoint slide between services: "Please turn off cell phones and pagers and set phasers to stun."***

WORSHIP

The worship portion should be about twenty-two minutes. (See chapter 3.)

TRANSITION

When it comes time for announcements, don't call them announcements.[6] And don't refer to the newcomers as visitors. This transition time is your chance to talk to newcomers. Include them right from their first time among you by calling them newcomers. Assume that the newcomers are "one of us." In general, the way you treat newcomers will determine whether or not you move from the struggling-sized church to the Perfectly Imperfect Church.

Say, "If you are a first-time newcomer with us today, I hope you feel entirely at home. We would love to get your name just to know that you were among us today and to send you a little bit of information about us. We promise that we won't overwhelm you with information or bug you. No one will show up unannounced at your door."

Note: *Never make newcomers stand up.* The only people new to a church who like to stand up are highly entrenched church people.

Anyone who is slightly introverted or uncomfortable or unsure of the entire experience not only will not stand up, but will make a careful note that this is *not* a safe place. That newcomer will not return.

As you make plugs (announcements) for upcoming events, remember that you're speaking to the entire congregation. Don't plug these events as if you're talking to a small family, and don't plug events that apply only to a small portion of the gathered church. Talking about these events tells newcomers, "We are oriented toward 'us' not 'you.' "

Take an offering. Take one offering. Don't make too much of a production of the offering. Newcomers and money do mix, but you have to be graceful when presenting the topic.

General guidelines for welcoming newcomers:

- Don't over-ask for money.
- Treat first-time people as newcomers, not as visitors, from the beginning.
- Seek to assimilate them right away through heartfelt, intelligent interaction.
- Don't embarrass them.

VIDEO/DRAMA/LIVE STORIES

An effective service needs something to connect with the people between worship and the message. This can be either a setup for the message or a stand-alone humor piece that adds to the total atmosphere. I'm big on building atmosphere, so I'm inclined to do humorous pieces most of the time.

You will have to choose between video and drama. For years we tried to no avail to use drama. It was always corny. Frankly, most of the drama I see in churches as I travel is every bit as corny and overdone as what we experienced. Each time I see a church drama, I think, *Now I remember why we stopped doing drama!*

I am biased toward the use of homegrown videos. Video does have its advantages over live performances. For example, it's precise—you know exactly what you are getting. Live performances vary in time and quality. People are conditioned to watch a video. Video allows for a lot more creativity than live performance. Video can be done anywhere there's a screen and a projector, or even a television and VCR in smaller settings. It can be done again and again.

MESSAGE

Twenty-five to thirty minutes is about as long as people can endure a message. I know from listening to the tapes of well-known pastors from around the country that it is common for weekend messages to run forty-five minutes. It works for them, perhaps, but it isn't a good practice for someone who isn't an advanced or highly gifted speaker. As a rule of thumb, if you have just twenty minutes of message to give, then speak for twenty minutes. To limit your speaking time requires significant self-control, but with a little practice, you can do it.

CLOSE

Give people an opportunity to respond to Christ.

I do this in a number of different ways. One is the "Look up if you'd like to make a faith commitment" approach. If people are holding hands, I ask them to squeeze the hands of the people next to them if they just responded to Christ. This approach is a great way to launch a discipleship relationship with the new follower and a more mature Christian.

Another approach is to simply close the service with a special prayer. I say, "Today if God got your attention for the first time and you are feeling as though God is inviting you to follow him, you need to take note of that. He can get your attention in many ways—through the worship, through a prayer, through reading the Bible, or through something that was said. If somehow God spoke to you for the first time, that's a signal that you need to respond to him. Pray this with me. Say this simple prayer as a way of presenting yourself to God: 'Well, God, here I am.' "

> ***It's no wonder we struggle with simplicity. We live in an anti-simple society and in a time of complexity. We have developed amazing numbers***

> ***of choices. I've heard you can now choose from 750 kinds of cars, and I've counted 25 types of Kleenex, and over 43 kinds of Snapple tea.***

Simple Discovery:
Simplicity = focus.

One of the church planters I'm working with told me recently that he has three cards in his pocket, each labeled with one of the three things he's working on—outreach, celebrations, and small groups. He gave each of his leaders a recipe box with three index cards in it, and the cards were labeled with the same three priorities. I think he has the right idea. Working on just those priorities, he'll have his hands full for the next several years, perhaps for the next decade. What a contrast his approach is to the complex "we have to be good at a bunch of things" approach taken by so many new churches. If he succeeds in those three areas, he will have a great church.

Simple Discovery:
Simplifying = saying no to many good things.

To simplify you have to choose to do some things and choose to not do some things that are currently on your plate. For most of us, choosing the top three priorities, and truly giving ourselves to those priorities, means we are going to have to *un*-choose about sixty-seven other things on our plates.

For me it was my beloved Friday night seminars. I had conducted a series of equipping seminars on Friday nights for some time. They were fairly well attended. They made me feel good because I got lots of strokes when I did them. The people who attended them liked them. Plus they were fun. I'm not sure where they fell when I numbered my priorities, but they weren't in the top three. When I became ruthless with my simplification agenda, the Friday seminars fell somewhere between priority number four and priority number seventy, so they had to go.

Simple Discovery:
Simplifying = pain.

You have to get to the "I quit" stage before you can become truly simple. Getting simple is unbelievably painful and difficult. As I look back at my venture through leadership, I see many "I quit" episodes. At the time they seemed simply painful, chaotic, and meaningless. Now as I reflect back on them, I realize that they were in fact times of greater and greater simplification. I was becoming more and more effective at each turn in the road.

Simple Discovery:
The most important word in simple is no.

You don't have the resources to do more than three things, nor do you have the time, so you're going to have to be a person who has the courage to say no. You have to be the person who decides what the list of three is going to be. If you listen to all the people in your world telling you what the three things are, your list will be 173 items long.

Imagine you're growing a fruit tree. If you prune the tree properly, it will bear more fruit. If you look at churches that grow from one hundred to two hundred, or from the two-hundred level to the Perfectly Imperfect Church size (three to five hundred), they became increasingly simple at every step along the way.

My concern with the amazing number of church-building how-to books is that each offers such clearly defined answers in neat packages. The books allow little "wiggle room" for the reader, little room to deviate and listen to the Spirit. In their attempts to help others find the way forward, some authors have introduced another layer of complication. They have muddied the waters and made the difficult task of navigation even more difficult. We need to keep it simple.

HOW TO MOVE YOUR GROUP TOWARD SIMPLICITY

- Shorten your services to sixty minutes.
- Treat newcomers right.

- Aspire to be simple and effective.
- Have plenty of signs to direct people.
- Carefully define yourself with your list of three things.

ENDNOTES

1. N.T. Wright, *The Challenge of Jesus* (Downers Grove, IL: InterVarsity Press, 1999), 43-44.
2. "One Small Pennsylvania Town Taking Notice of Itinerant Preacher Who Calls Himself What's Your Name," *Good Morning America* (ABC News, Feb. 16, 2000).
3. "Fern High School Janitor George Smith Gives School Their Commencement Speech," *Today Show* (NBC News, May 29, 2001).
4. You can check out their passionate love for skipping at their Web site—www.iskip.com.
5. George Barna, *Re-Churching the Unchurched* (Ventura, CA: Issachar Resources, 2000), 25.
6. I recommend using the term *plugs*. The word *announcements* sounds like you are about to waste the time of everyone listening. As the camp song goes, "Announcements, announcements, announcements—what a terrible way to die..."

Path 2: UPWARD

It was Sunday night. My wife and I had driven more than an hour to get to the crowded Southern California gymnasium. On the drive, I asked myself more than once why I was driving so far when I was already tired to go to something out of the way like this. Even though we got there ten minutes early, finding a parking space was difficult. After the long trek into the building, the only seats my wife and I could find were the cheap ones where the temperature hovered in the upper nineties. The place smelled like sweat. It reminded me of a PE class!

The worship leaders in this volunteer band were decent musicians, but not spectacularly skilled. They were very casually dressed. Some wore shorts. Several wore beach clothes and no shoes.

The songs were easy to follow, and there was something unique about them. For one thing, they were written in the first person, and they were directed to God. They weren't about God; they weren't directed to the people. For another, they were sung with passion and heartfelt fervor. The enthusiasm was contagious!

Soon I felt a spectacular and profound presence of God in the room. It was like nothing I had experienced before. People's reactions to God's presence varied: Some wept, others lifted their hands in the air, and still others sat in absolute silence, not wanting to disturb the manifest presence of God's Spirit.

That was my first experience with transcendent worship, worship that goes beyond songs that are well-executed or diligently sung to an interaction with the Holy Spirit. Transcendence is getting beyond singing songs to encountering God through them. It makes all the difference in the world when it comes to worship.

Power Principle: *Change the struggling-church mind-set in worship.*

It is absolutely essential to do worship well from the beginning of your church's existence. It's what people experience first when they come to your celebration. Newcomers will judge your church by your worship. Even those who don't participate in the worship will "feel you out" and make judgments about the quality and philosophy of your church's ministry based on their first twenty minutes with you. If they like other aspects of your service but don't like your worship, they most likely won't be back.

Here's a caution for smaller churches: You have to get past acting like a small family during worship. The natural tendency for small, struggling churches is to do what they call family-friendly worship, which means that children are present with the adults during the singing portion of the service. I don't recommend including the children. They don't get much out of worship, in spite of what we adults would like to think. It just isn't fair to the children; they are bored being with the adults, and they are not learning to worship. They would be far better off in another room with children their own age. Overall, children will have a more positive experience at church if they spend the hour with other children. In my interactions with churches during the past twenty years, I have never seen a church do worship well when the children were present.

Power Principle: *Find "Big God's" presence.*

It is essential that we encounter God—Big God's big presence—when we gather in worship.

I call it Big God's presence because that's what God's manifest life feels like when we are in the midst of it. I have felt the lack of God's presence in worship many times: "small God," if you will. I don't want to have a worship experience again without the full, manifest presence of God upon our time together.

Great worship isn't about doing brilliant things or finding brilliant and highly gifted people to lead the music ministry. Great worship is about simple God encounters. It begins with inviting the Holy Spirit to be upon our worship time and expressing to God our great desire to simply be with him.

Before this can happen, we need to identify the obstacles that prevent our experiencing God when we gather. A great worship encounter with Big God is never so much about doing everything right as it is about clearing the distractions from worship.

If you want to remove distractions, one simple rule of thumb is, to put it plainly: *Don't do goofy things during worship.* In struggling churches, it often happens that someone suddenly feels led by God's Spirit to do silly things during worship. I have found that unplanned inspirations nearly always backfire and ostracize all of the levelheaded newcomers present.

For example, I recently watched as the worship leader of a struggling church acted on an uninspired idea without clearing it with the senior pastor. He said, "Isn't it great that we're all one extended family here? Let's all come up on the stage and stand here together and worship together." Everyone attending—about 120 people, including several newcomers—dutifully came up to the stage. Everyone was uncomfortable. The goofy idea ostracized all of the newcomers. (By the way, I disagree that a church is one big extended family. The use of such terms is a sure sign that a church is stuck in the struggling-church stage, and it creates a negative effect on newcomers.)

An obstacle can be as simple as singing one song too many—singing five songs when four songs would have been just right. An obstacle might be the worship team gathering in a huddle on the stage to pray before a service. The huddle-prayer draws attention to the worship team members, making them look like they want to appear extra-spiritual. It's cheerleading from the front instead of leading the group into God's presence through worship. Prayer before worship is great, but the worship team should gather to pray behind closed doors.

In the end, though, we can analyze technical elements of the worship after the weekend celebration, and we can plan to have skilled musicians galore for next week's celebration. But neither analysis nor plans will make a bit of difference if we don't profoundly and consistently meet God in worship when we gather.

> ***"My theory is this: God goes where he's wanted. That's a scary thought in a country like the United States, home to a robust economy and 500 satellite TV channels for diversion and entertainment, not to mention Disney World."*** [1]
>
> —Philip Yancey

Power Principle:
Avoid complicated worship.

When you choose songs for your worship, check them against this list. Are they

- catchy,
- memorable,
- simple enough to hear once and learn,
- enjoyable to sing, and
- do the songs express the heart of the church?

Consider writing your own songs if you have talented musicians. Homegrown songs can inspire powerful worship. Since the church is a living entity, it is natural that we will receive songs from the Spirit that reflect what God is doing in our lives.

At some point early on, you need to decide if you are going to have piano-based or guitar-based worship. From my experience it is easier to go with guitar-centered worship. The guitar is easy to follow in worship. Ultimately the question of guitar versus piano is a style question, but if talent is in limited supply then guitar worship might be the way to go. There are many more adequate guitar worship leaders out there than piano worship leaders. Whichever type of instrumentation you choose, you can reduce complexity by keeping your worship set all in the same key or by singing several songs in the same key before changing.

ASSEMBLING A BAND

If I were putting together a worship band, I would begin with a lead singer who plays guitar or piano and then add the following in this order:

Bass guitar: A bass guitar helps singers follow along. It doesn't draw a lot of attention to itself, so you might not realize how much it helps you. But when the bass is removed, it is difficult to sing along.

Second voice: If you have two singers, having one of each gender usually works best.

Electric guitar: An electric guitar adds fullness to your sound. Find someone who can play subtly. Overplaying the electric guitar distracts from the worship and draws attention to the guitar. This musician needs to blend in and play filler material, not lead licks.

Third voice: More voices add more depth to the vocal sound.

Keyboards: Keyboards, like the electric guitar, back up the lead instrument.

Drums and percussion: Drums can do a lot of good in the right hands, but they can be distracting in the wrong hands. Find someone who has a light touch.

VIDEO EVALUATION

Every so often, I have someone videotape our worship set, from the welcome to the ending prayer. Another camera captures the facial reactions of people in the congregation so we can see how engaged people are at various points of the service. Then I watch the video—as painful as that may be—with our worship leaders. We pause the tape frequently to pick up on the good points and to see how we could improve various aspects of the worship set. It's almost always a great learning time. I recommend you try it.

Another way to simplify is to keep the focus on the music. Talking between songs tends to get in the way of worship. Those who have come to worship have come to sing to God, not to hear quips or admonitions from a worship leader who is trying to cheer the crowd forward. I also include prayer in this moratorium. If you chose to include prayer, make it short and sweet (and scripted, if need be, to keep it on track).

I've found that the worship experience is usually more authentic if the worship leader plays an instrument. Otherwise the worship leader seems to be performing more than leading worship. When the worship leader plays an instrument, the entire equation changes.

Power Principle: *Avoid letting worship run too long.*

For some people, worship is an acquired taste. It's like coffee: At first taste, it may not go down all that great, but the flavor has a way of growing on you. Some people can enjoy a lengthy worship time, but usually the uninitiated can't appreciate a long swig of the good stuff. I can worship for a couple of hours without growing weary, but I've had to work my way up to that level.

We were at one time a "high worship" church. That is, we would sing worship choruses for up to forty-five minutes. However, the long worship time made our church "seeker-hostile." Our attitude was, "If those new people can't handle the presence of God in large doses, well, that's *their* problem!" The long worship worked fine for us, but for those who hadn't developed a taste for worship, it was too long.

As more and more newcomers found their way into our midst, I began to feel that we were overdoing our worship, that perhaps we had created an insiders-only club. So I began to do some research. I stood off to the side of church sanctuaries across America and observed how long the worship endurance of congregations was. I found the same result in almost every congregation, regardless of denominational background, tradition, or stated values. People are capable of being engaged in worship for a maximum of about twenty-two minutes. After twenty-two minutes, most worshippers' attention span drops significantly. Needless to say, we made a shift to a twenty-two-minute worship set, though it caused some consternation for a time among people who love to worship. But now participation in worship is on a significantly higher level than it was before we shortened worship.

OUR HURRY-UP WORLD

We live in a hurry-up world. Columnist Dan Kadison noted that the producers of the 2001 Oscar-awards show offered a large-screen, high-definition television to the winner with the shortest reception speech. Julia Roberts said "no thanks" to the television offer; she said that, since she already had a nice television, she chose to talk for a while. Michael De Wit, winner of the Best Animated Short, spoke for only fifteen seconds and won the television. Still, no one topped Alfred Hitchcock's classic "Thank you" at the 1967 awards show. [2]

Power Principle:
Focus.

Who are we singing to? What are we singing about?

People need a transition from the parking lot to the presence of God, from their week into God's throne room. Worship can provide that transition if you start by singing songs *about* God and transitions to songs *addressed to* God.

People come to worship because they want to experience God. Anything that doesn't help people feel God's presence is probably a distraction. I've seen many things distract from worship, such as worship dance, worship flag waving (I nearly had my eye poked out), worship jumping, and worship calisthenics. The activities were no doubt intended to help worship, but in the end they were clutter that got in the way of people seeing God more clearly.

At the same time, I think we need to be more expressive in worship, not less expressive. One woman I know lost interest in attending church as a young girl because, after she danced one morning in church, she was informed that church was no place for dancing. She said she wanted nothing to do with a God who would be offended by her worship dance.

Creative forms of expression are great as long as they are truly expressive for those worshipping. People doing their thing off to the side while the rest of the church serves as impassive observers can have a negative effect. Unless people are engaged, creative expressions can distract them from the centrality of worship.

We gather to have an experience with Big God. We gather together to transcend our week and experience a time of intimacy with God. That's the goal of all our worship experiences. The simpler the better. The less clutter the better.

As a rule of thumb, if something strikes you as distracting, it probably is. We ought to pay more attention to our hunches. We would stay out of the weeds more often. Doing what makes sense is always better than doing what is mystical, no matter how spiritual it may seem on the surface.

Power Principle: *Worship opens the door to evangelism.*

Are you aware of the intricate connection between worship and evangelism? There is great power in worship. Without the significant touch of God's Spirit in worship, evangelism in a celebration service probably won't succeed. I have experienced this time and again. When I pray with people making a faith commitment to Christ during a service, I make direct reference to worship as the sign that God is real and calling them to follow. At the end of a service I will pray in response to the message, then I will say, "Some of you felt God's presence for the first time today. It likely happened as we were singing the worship songs earlier. If somehow God got your attention, if somehow he reached out and touched your life, make note of that right now. If that happened to you, that was God's way of prompting you to follow him." Then I lead them in a prayer to begin to follow Christ.

Something special happens at the emotional and visceral level when we pour out our hearts in worship to God. When not-yet-Christian people are in the room with already-Christian people, even the non-Christians are touched by the overflow of that atmosphere. They are drawn to Christ.

BREADTH VERSUS DEPTH

Although about eighty-two percent of Americans say they want to "experience spiritual growth, they lack the spiritual practices and disciplines that will take them there," according to The Arizona Republic newspaper, which quoted *Surveying the Religious Landscape*, a recent book by pollster George Gallup Jr. and consultant D. Michael Lindsay.

" 'Spirituality in America may be three thousand miles wide, but it remains only three inches deep' wrote Gallup, whose institute has surveyed Americans' religious beliefs and practices for sixty years." [3]

Power Principle: *Your style is not the key to success.*

Your church will be identified by your style of worship. People say,

"Oh, you're the rock-and-roll church," "You're the contemporary church," or "You're the acoustic-sounding church." You may even hear "Your worship sounds like the Dave Matthews Band." (Some people may take offense if their worship is compared to a secular band, but such comparisons are inevitable and, deep down, complimentary.)

At first glance, your worship style may seem to be the key to your success. After all, it's *your* sound. It's what people in your city associate with your church. You are highly invested in that sound.

In reality, great churches across America have sounds and styles that are very different from yours. Some churches are growing like weeds with a sound that couldn't be any more counter to your contemporary sound. I visited a church that claimed to hold contemporary worship, but people were singing thirty-five-year-old Bill Gaither songs. I like those songs just fine, but they are not contemporary worship songs. Granted, compared to hymns from the Reformation, they are renewal songs and are contemporary. That church in Southern California is growing nicely. It is a Perfectly Imperfect Church, which could soon be a Launching-Pad Church. The people know who they are, and they are being that enthusiastically.

Your style isn't what causes God's presence to come into your midst. Style is almost irrelevant. God comes into your midst because hearts are hungry for the presence of God.

CONTEMPORARY WORSHIP STYLES APPEAL TO NEW MEMBERS

"Protestant groups that have emphasized contemporary worship and electronic musical instruments, rather than traditional forms, show a dramatic increase in their appeal to new members," according to the Hartford Institute for Religion Research at the Hartford Seminary in Connecticut. However, transition to contemporary music can be a struggle. The institute conducted a sweeping study of forty-one religious denominations and faith groups and presented the results in *Faith Communities Today.* [4]

Power Principle:
Don't be completely original.

As someone once said, "There once was a man who said, 'I will be original or nothing.' In the end he became both."

There are lots of great models for worship out there. To get your worship going, find one and copy it. Consider setting up your band the way your model does it. Choose the same songs if you like the sound. If you like the way the guitars sound, strive for that same sound. Don't feel bad about copying someone else's worship style. If the truth be told, the worship group you're copying probably wasn't original to begin with either. Most likely, that group adopted a number of styles over a period of time and the conglomeration of those styles is what you see in front of you. There's nothing new under the sun. You don't have to write your own songs. You don't even have to have your own style. Done correctly, the song "Jesus Loves Me" works wonderfully!

On the other hand...

Power Principle:
Don't blindly copy someone else.

While choosing a pattern to follow is helpful in the beginning, eventually a church's worship will need to become its own. A church needs to connect to its city in its own language and using a metaphor that makes sense in its setting.

I've seen seeker-targeted churches imitate worship that they've seen—complete with choreographed movements and headset microphones—only to end up with what I call Up with People worship.[5] They're imitating in a not-so-effective way something they've seen at a big conference. It doesn't work, and it's not worshipful.

Don't be afraid to be different, but be aware that people grow weary of too much experimentation. Your church will eventually find its own sound, style, and focus. Find it and be that.

Power Principle:
Do a quality job, but don't obsess.

Nothing will kill the spirit of worship faster than an obsessive, perfectionist worship leader who is so detail-oriented that he or she can only see the "mistakes" being made and misses what God is doing in the service.

The goal of worship must be that everyone be aware of the manifest presence of God in our midst. There's a time to prepare diligently, and there's a time to let things flow and enjoy the presence of God. Once a service has started, it's time to get out of the way and enjoy God. There's little that can be done to change things at that point, except to make note of what goes wrong and plan to fix it by next week.

HOW TO BECOME MORE UPWARD-FOCUSED

- **Pay attention to flow.**

Be aware of flow from one song to the next. Sing several songs in the same key before transitioning to another key. The same rule holds true for tempo and pitch. It's fine to vary the tempo, but going back and forth too much confuses people and disturbs an atmosphere of worship. I like to start out with an upbeat song that is about God rather than directed to God. We use this first song as something of a call to worship—to get everyone on the same page in worship. Then we transition into slower songs that are directed to God. We typically finish a worship set with another worship song that is upbeat and declarative—that is, more about God. We have tasted and seen that the Lord is good, so we sing about that.

- **Be deliberate in your song choices.**

Choose songs written in keys that everyone can sing. Some choruses and hymns are written in such high keys that they are very difficult, for men in particular, to sing. It's no wonder men often complain that they don't like to sing at church. They get a sore throat from trying to sing songs in unrealistic keys! Before you decide to include a song in your stable of songs, you might test it by asking some men to sing it.

- **Keep things moving.**

Dead space between songs is not good. Transitions between upbeat songs and quiet songs can be difficult. Filling that space appropriately can be uncomfortable, but it is necessary.

- **Grow your worship.**

The more you grow, the less room there is for mistakes. What is forgivable when you have one hundred people might stand out as a glaring mistake when you have three hundred. It is imperative that you grow the worship as the church grows numerically.

- **Have musicians play within their skill levels.**

If your musicians are proficient in only three chords, then stay within that realm. Be aware that the more instruments you add, the more skill the leader and other players will need.

- **Know who's leading.**

Don't enlist a worship leader unless you know the person will be good at the job. A great worship leader should have humility, skill, and a philosophy of ministry that's in sync with the direction of the church.

- **Choose musicians carefully.**

Avoid husband and wife combinations in the band; if you have difficulties with one you've lost the other as well.

- **Be aware of your musician pool.**

When a musician starts attending your church, pay attention to that person. You will have to draw on your pool from time to time.

- **Promote from within.**

Homegrown worship leaders are usually the best leaders. Finding a worship leader in your congregation can be a lot easier than hiring from outside. However homegrown worship leaders take longer to train.

- **Keep musical skill in focus.**

The ideal worship leader is a skilled musician who has been taught to worship, not the reverse.

- **Make everyone feel included.**

Struggling churches have exclusive worship—more like the worship that takes place in a small group. Perfectly Imperfect Churches have inclusive worship—worship that allows everyone to feel at home.

- **Start small.**

Having worship led by one decent guitarist with a decent voice is better than trying to create a slick, pop-band appearance. Authenticity is far better than slick professionalism.

ENDNOTES

1. Philip Yancey, "God at Large," Christianity Today (February 5, 2001), 136.
2. Dan Kadison, "Hey, Wait a Minute, Who the Heck Won That TV?" The New York Post (March 27, 2001), 7.
3. Kelly Ettenborough, "Where Has God Gone?" The Arizona Republic (February 25, 2001), J1.
4. *Faith Communities Today*, Hartford Institute for Religion Research, Hartford Seminary. See www.fact.hartsem.edu
5. "Up with People" was a musical group that toured the country during the protest era of the '60s and '70s. The group tried to be uplifting with a message of "positivity," but most people found the group about as authentic as The Brady Bunch at a Jimi Hendrix concert.

Paths to the Perfectly Imperfect Church

Path 3: OUTWARD

Betsy and Sally don't look wild and crazy, but they are revolutionaries. They're moms who are out to change the world! One Saturday not long ago, they were out with a band of servant evangelists on a unique mission: They were going door-to-door giving away toilet paper! As people came to their doors, the team said, "Hi! We're giving away free toilet paper to show Christ's love in a practical way."

Most people would smile and say, "Thanks. We already have toilet paper."

Then the servant evangelists would respond, "Yes, but this is Christian toilet paper! We're giving it in the name of Christ." Then they would offer to pray about anything that was going on in the people's lives.

At one door, a woman accepted the toilet paper but said she didn't want prayer. Then as the Betsy and Sally stepped away from the porch, she stopped them: "Wait a minute. Are you the kind of Christians that believe in prayer? I need some." They assured her they were that kind of Christian. The woman immediately burst into tears. "I recently had an abortion. I know it was a mistake, and I can't believe that God would forgive me for this." She was sobbing so deeply that she couldn't speak.

Betsy and Sally prayed for the peace of God to come upon this woman. They prayed for forgiveness. They unrolled some of the toilet paper and used it to dab her eyes. As the weeping subsided, they were able to counsel her.

"You know, you really need to come and hang out with us at church. You'd really like it. It's laid back. The messages are practical. The music is good. The coffee is hot. We think it would change your life," Betsy said.

"Oh, I couldn't come," she said. "My kids are out of control. They aren't 'church-broken.' "

"That's OK. They sound like my kids. You bring them and meet me by the door."

Up or Out?

I don't know which comes first—looking upward or looking outward. Sometimes having a dynamic worship experience makes us fall more deeply in love with Christ, which causes us to reach out to the not-yet-Christians God wants to include in his family. But sometimes it's looking outward first that leads us to worship—as we love the lost, we feel a need to worship God.

Worship and evangelism are knit together at the core. Both are on the nerve path that conducts feelings to the deepest recesses of the heart.

People are afraid to be outward. The E word scares them. What images come to your mind when you think of evangelism? The church that seeks to become a Perfectly Imperfect Church will need to address this issue.

> *"There is no revolution that has ever taken place that can be compared with the one which has been produced by the words of Jesus Christ."*
> —Mark Hopkins, former president of Williams College

Christ Calls Us to a Revolution.

To address evangelism properly, a little bit of change here and a little bit of change there won't do. We need a full-scale revolution. And every good revolution needs a good focusing statement. In radical circles, that statement is called a manifesto.

Here's ours:

> A Pretty Good Manifesto
> *"We exist to love our city into relationship with Christ."*

It's just ten words.

The leaders of nearly every church say they want to reach out, but few know the first thing about how to start. The Pretty Good Church is committed to doing basic, low-risk, yet effective ways of reaching out that just about anyone in the congregation can do—and will want to do.

A good manifesto needs practical handles people can grab onto. In this chapter, I will give guidelines for outreach that will help you build a Perfectly Imperfect Church.

1. OUTWARDNESS COMES IN A LOT OF PACKAGES.

Servant evangelism (doing acts of kindness and generosity to show people the love of Christ), caring for the poor, and planting new churches constitute the language of outreach that I speak fluently. Outreach is like a tool belt full of tools. Being effective means learning how to use a variety of tools and having the wisdom to pull out the right tool at the right time to meet the evangelistic need at hand. The key to making evangelism work is being faithful to carry out the approach for the long run.

"I'M GLAD YOU ASKED"

Singapore is a "fine city"—that is, there are hefty fines for dozens of things we see as acceptable in the United States. Fines are levied for infractions such as chewing gum or sharing your faith with someone of another belief system. However, if someone asks about your faith, you are free to answer his or her questions. Christians in this small, multicultural city-country are increasingly using servant evangelism to get around this problem of sharing their faith. When they serve others with an act of kindness and generosity, Hindus, Muslims, and Buddhists ask, "So why are you being to nice to me?" To that they say, "I'm glad you asked…"

2. ALL EVANGELISM IS GOOD EVANGELISM…

…as long as it's respectful of the individual. Any sort of evangelism can abuse people and therefore be less than positive.

I am partial to servant evangelism, but I also enjoy knocking on doors now and then and using more direct approaches to sharing the good news of Christ with people. The point, regardless of the approach, is to "love" people into relationship with Christ.

MUSCULAR CHRISTIANITY

"The Bible teaches its followers to turn the other cheek. Then again, its authors had never heard of the Christian Wrestling Federation, where the meek are blessed with bone-rattling body slams and headfirst flips through the ring ropes."

The CWF brings its fans action-packed matches featuring Apocalypse, Angel, the Beast, and Jesus Freak. "It also brings something else—a message of faith and hope." This Texas-based group of about a dozen wrestlers is touring the state with a program of matches followed by the gospel message. A CWF founder explained that the group cares about ministry first. Wrestling is simply a way to reach teens. [1]

3. LEADING OTHERS TO CHRIST ISN'T THAT COMPLICATED.

When I first received Christ, I did so on my own, quietly. No one had ever explained to me how this process was supposed to take place. My homespun prayer was similar to what the Bible tells us the prophets said when they encountered God's presence. I prayed simply, "Well, God, here I am." It was a prayer of deep surrender, and it was wonderfully effective at introducing me to the person of Christ.

A few weeks later, I explained to some other Christians how I had come to know Christ. They were aghast that I had not put my faith in Christ in the prescribed manner—the official "way that every one receives Christ," as my friends said.

Lately, however, I've been rethinking the way we introduce people to Christ. I'm moving from a "tell 'em how it is" to a "let's discover salvation together" mode.

"I want people to get past the idea that they understand Christianity because they went to Sunday school. You have to learn how to do it. You have to undergo an apprenticeship. Nobody really wants to love their neighbor as themselves."

—Stanley Hauerwas, professor of divinity and law at Duke University [2]

How to Nudge Someone to Christ

I allow myself to be a witness-in-progress.

I describe myself as someone who is still discovering salvation. Even though I've clearly come to know Christ already, it's important that I not come across as being in the company of the arrived.

I was on a plane recently, writing on my computer. My computer is colorful, and the lady sitting next to me commented on that. We began to chat. She asked what I wrote about, and I said simply, "People."

She said, "Well, it looks like you write about God. You aren't a Christian, are you?"

"Yes, but not that kind. You see, I've been a Christian for twenty-five years, but I'm still not very good at it. I'm still practicing quite a bit."

After we had talked for quite awhile about what it means to practice following Christ—that he's pleased with our willingness to follow him with a good effort—she admitted she was attracted to the image of Christ that I presented.

Eventually she said, "This sort of Jesus I could get into—the kind that lets you practice. You know, if we were flying to Hawaii instead of Seattle, I think I might be persuaded to become one of you."

I also help people present themselves to God.

Most people are intimidated by the idea of praying with someone to express faith in Christ. In some faith traditions, making a faith commitment is not emphasized. Language aside, many adults—even in church circles—have not clarified their relationships with Christ. They might have a childlike faith in God in general but not have a specific, spelled-out relationship with Jesus Christ. The physical, emotional, or psychological needs of those we encounter are important, but the experience of clarifying one's relationship with Christ meets a need in a class all by itself! Knowing that you are going to heaven radically changes your entire outlook on life.

Recently, a significant survey at Vineyard Community Church in Cincinnati gathered data on the topic of evangelism, and I discovered several encouraging truths. First, I found that about 60 percent of the people surveyed are excited about sharing their faith. Second, most of the people surveyed (75 percent) have shared their faith on a regular basis (three to four times in the past six months). The attendees of VCC are average people. While the percentage of people who share their faith may be higher than might be normal in other churches, I suspect that Christians would like to see this degree of evangelism in every church. The survey also found that, even when so many people are sharing their faith, people feel they are being held back from sharing their faith by a fear of rejection and a lack of training.

With these things in mind, here are a few principles I keep in mind as I try to lead others to Christ.

KEEP IT LOVING.

Don't be pushy. Approaching someone with a message of love and an aggressive attitude doesn't make sense. Unfortunately the combination is found too often in evangelism.

KEEP IT REAL.

When you introduce Christ to spiritual explorers, guide them first to a place of discovery. Then direct them in a simple prayer of presentation—"*Well, God, here I am...*" You may want to pray more extensively with them later.

KEEP IT STRAIGHT.

Here's the message:

- God is for you.
- God forgives me and you.
- God can change me and you.

When sharing my faith, I first say that God can forgive and change me. I keep the focus on my weakness and stay far from the brokenness of others. Spiritual explorers are sensitive to anything that suggests an accusation or spiritual one-upmanship.

KEEP IT SIMPLE.

Remember—the main thing is to keep the main thing the main thing. I'm all for training, as long as it's reasonable. You can find many programs designed to help Christians share their faith. Just be careful not to make it too complicated or too lengthy.

DEFINE *NORMAL* AS IT APPLIES TO OUTREACH.

If we don't specify what the desired norm looks like, we will forever operate in a hit-or-miss mode. In my interaction with churches, I have asked if going out into the community once per month to do outreach is reasonable. Consistently I hear that it is. So we might say that normal outreach is monthly.

However you define *normal*, your leaders must act according to that definition. Ultimately the members of your church will only do what your leaders *do*, not what they *say*. Therefore, it is vital that the leaders of your church, especially the senior leader, buy into outreach as an ongoing value. If the senior leader is going out once per month with the membership, word will spread that it is normal to do outreach in this church.

Another aspect of outreach normalcy is financing. If outreach is truly a value in your church, it needs to be supported by budgeted money. Inadequate financial backing is common when a church starts outreach in a serious way. If you are jumping into evangelism in a big way—especially into servant evangelism, which can be a bit pricey—it is OK at first to seek financing from individual benefactors, such as businessmen in the church. Ultimately the church needs to get behind the efforts of the outreach activities.

Ask small groups to do an outreach every fourth to sixth time they meet. Encourage the groups to establish a regular outreach schedule so that outreach becomes part of the small-group culture.

DEFINING OUTREACH AS NORMAL AND FUN

The North American Mission Board of the Southern Baptist Convention sponsors summer Epic Adventures, which are servant evangelism outreaches to major cities across the United States. Epic Adventures, which is promoted as a "non-threatening but high-impact" way to share Jesus, is getting a healthy number of takers to sign up! [3]

BE CONSISTENT IN YOUR OUTREACHES.

Do your "rounds." Just as a doctor sees his patients regularly, you need to decide what your territory is and get around in that area on a regular basis—even if going out means that you and your spouse go by yourselves to hand out bottles of water to show Christ's love. The battle will be won by those who are most consistent. The difference between growing and static movements always comes down to consistency.

TELL ENCOURAGING STORIES OFTEN.

You'll build credibility each time you tell others in your church about an outreach experience. If possible relate an outreach story at each service or at least once per month. If you have video capabilities, tape your outreaches and show footage with some musical background.

A BICYCLE, A BROOM AND A BIBLE

Romain Joyce ministers from a bicycle to people from all walks of life. According to an article in the Charlotte Observer, the sixty-something preacher has ridden through the streets of Mount Airy, North Carolina, since 1996, balancing a broom and a Bible on his Fury Spectra ten-speed. He rides where Jesus tells him to, he said, and cleans sidewalks as well as people's hearts, he hopes.

Joyce keeps a note pad with him to record prayer requests. He said that mostly people want to talk about marriage problems or addiction.

Sweeping and ministering full time has always been a dream, he said. "The first time I did it, I found out God had a lot of hard work for me to do; I do the ministry every day when I can." [4]

FIND CREATIVE WAYS TO MAKE OUTREACH PROMINENT AT WEEKEND CELEBRATIONS.

Present lots of opportunities for outreach involvement. Set up a table near the exit and supply it with outreach materials. For example, set out squeegees and window cleaner so that people can take the supplies with them to do their own outreach that week. Or provide bottles of water people can give away. Be sure to provide connection cards. Each "touch" of God's love should be accompanied by a card that includes the church's logo and service times, a map, and a short message, such as, "This really is free! It's a small way to say, 'God loves you.' No strings attached! If we can be of more help, please give us a call." The connection cards provide a means of following up once people have been touched with the love of Christ.

STAY INVOLVED IN SOCIAL OUTREACH.

According to Scripture, caring for the needy isn't optional. God has given us a heart for the "least of these" so that we will reach out to them in increasingly creative ways. It is important that we consider ministry to the needy a normal part of the budget so that it continues as an ongoing ministry.

OUTREACH AND GROWTH

Half of this country's religious congregations are growing and thriving, especially those that embrace social outreach, according to Associated Press writer Verena Dobnik's article about the comprehensive study completed by the Hartford Institute for Religion Research at Hartford Seminary in Connecticut.

According to the study of 14,301 houses of worship in 41 faith groups, a primary factor contributing to growth was social ministries that reach out to the poor. Most congregations offer a food pantry, more than one in three offer tutoring for youth, and two in three sponsor a thrift shop. [5]

"TANGIBILIFY" THE GOSPEL OF CHRIST.

Tangibilify is a great word. It means that we need to make God's word real by walking it out in genuine ways. We must be a humble people who are self-deprecating and don't take ourselves too seriously. We must be the kind of people in the pew that people in the streets can relate to.

Great churches have a "whatever-it-takes" attitude. That's what we are doing when we make Christ tangible with every aspect of our lives.

OUTWARD UNIVERSITY STUDENTS

As a junior at Trinity College in Hartford, Connecticut, Carrie Haslett spent spring break in a beach resort in Fort Lauderdale, Florida. "We lived on the beach, drinking banana daiquiris the whole day," she recalled.

The next year, as a senior, Ms. Haslett, returned to Fort Lauderdale. This time she stayed in a musty cabin crammed with bunk beds and rose with the sun to hammer shingles onto a roof that would soon shelter a low-income family she has never met.

"This feels so good—to see the fruits of your labor so immediately is so gratifying," she said. "People here care more about doing something meaningful than they care about ...how good their tan is."

Carrie Haslett was one of sixty-seven students recruited by Habitat for Humanity's collegiate challenge. Other organizations also offer "alternative spring break" opportunities. In 2001, some thirty thousand students traveled to locales exotic and mundane, tutoring children, landscaping parks, building wheelchair ramps, cooking for the homeless and people with AIDS, settling refugees, leading rallies against gang violence, or painting murals on inner-city buildings. [6]

CREATE AN OUTREACH IDENTITY.

What's your outreach identity? It's your number one attractor. It's your primary credibility-gainer. Your outreach identity is more important than your worship identity. My primary approach to servant evangelism is cleaning toilets at gas stations and restaurants. I know others who rake leaves. Others give away sodas to show Christ's love. What do you do?

MAKE A STRONG AND ENDURING COMMITMENT TO OUTREACH.

In the ebb and flow of the body of Christ, it is easy to get caught up in smallness. Life happens, people talk, and occasionally there is controversy. Unless we are busy doing the outward will of God, we will inevitably fall prey to smallness of heart. We will get caught up in controversy and speculation about other parts of the church, and, in general, activities that are not redemptive and an utter waste of kingdom resources. Living out a life of commitment to outreach keeps us from much harm to ourselves and others.

HOW TO BECOME MORE OUTWARD

- Give people lots of chances to respond to the message of Christ in public settings. The more opportunities you provide, the more people will respond.
- Talk about and live out the value of outreach. If I were planting a church, I would have bottles of water by the door during the summer so that people could take the water with them to distribute in the community. I'd have rakes by the door in the fall.
- Even small churches need to talk about starting new churches. But don't try to do it until you have at least three hundred gathered at the home church.

ENDNOTES

1. Selwyn Crawford, "The Bible Belts: Christian wrestling makes clean break," The Dallas Morning News (May 12, 2000).
2. "Amen Corner: News and Notes," Atlanta Journal and Constitution (August 18, 2001), 2B.
3. Their Web site is: www.epicnow.org or call 800-264-5129.
4. Sherry Wilson, "With a Broom and a Bible, He Ministers," Winston-Salem Journal.
5. Verena Dobnik, "Study: Religious Congregations Rise," AP Online (March 13, 2001).
6. Jodi Wilgoren, "Helping Hands at Spring Break," The New York Times (March 22, 2001).

Path 4: ANOINTED

The two women sitting next to me on the airplane were curious about the people sitting around us who were excitedly talking about, of all things, going to the city dumps in Mexico City.

"Pardon me for asking, but I must have misheard," said one of the women. "I could have sworn that I heard some of your party say that you're going to the city dumps. That's not right is it?"

"Why, yes," I answered. "People from our church come down once a month to attend to the needs of people from the city dump."

"Why in the world would you do that?"

"We just think that this is the sort of thing that Jesus would do if he were walking around in the world today."

The two women explained that they were not churchgoing people at all. They were part of an international dance group that was gathering in Mexico City for a few days.

One of them said, "It's like you guys are doing the same work Jesus did, only in more places than he did it."

By the time we got off the plane, the women were so excited about what we were doing that they were ready to help support our efforts financially.

When I first came to Cincinnati, I drove around the city with an aching heart—aching to connect with just some of the 1.7 million people in our city. It was incredibly difficult to meet people in a strange city. The people I initially gathered were not well-connected within the city. Since they didn't have extensive community connections to draw from, I had to start from scratch to develop a vision for beginning a church.

I began to take note of the deeds of the kingdom of God as they are explained in the New Testament, particularly in the life and ministry of Jesus. Where those deeds are done, the kingdom of God comes. It took me awhile, but I began to see that the kingdom of God isn't a time or a place, but an atmosphere that comes upon us when we do the deeds of the kingdom.

One of the first things we did as a beginning church was to feed the hungry and "bring Christmas" to a group of needy families. About half of our little church—twelve in all—came together on Christmas Eve to give away food, Christmas gifts, and Christmas trees in a crack neighborhood.

The temperature that night was well below zero, but we saw children running around without coats and with shoes that showed bare skin through the gaping holes. We stood in freezing homes to pray for entire families, sometimes with the gas stove burners blazing at full flame as people attempted to heat their homes. We prayed with children and with wives whose husbands were in jail. Some people told us that we were the answer to prayer; they'd been praying that their kids would have a Christmas. Some pointed us to other families who were in greater need than they were. Our hearts were filled with love for these families.

During the next few weeks, people asked what was new at our church. It was natural for us to report what we had been doing. A businessman heard about what we were doing and was moved to give significantly to our outreach. More importantly, he began to talk to others about our efforts. For years after that, I heard from people he had told about our outreach. We made an impression.

> *I discovered an important lesson: It is better to be profound than to be clever.*

For years we tried using cleverness to start this church, but the results were minimal. No one listened to us. Then we started doing small, profound things—the simple things that Jesus did—and everything changed. Everyone was telling our story, and many were listening.

We have been at it steadily since then, and God has blessed our efforts. We have developed about three hundred serving projects that get people into the community. Through these projects, we are serving hundreds of thousands of people each year in practical ways, as well as touching the community of the needy. Now, after fifteen years in the city, we are known as the people who do acts of kindness and generosity. If you ask anyone in Cincinnati about the Vineyard Community Church, he or she will say, "They're the people who do the kindness stuff!" That's the sort of reputation you want to develop in your community.

Building Anointing

A positive perception in your community is more powerful than words, programs, slogans, and all the great sermons in the world. There is cute, and there is profound. To promote your church through conventional advertising is to be cute. Recently I saw a church sign that read, "C-H-C-H—What's Missing? U-R." Groaners like this abound in the church world, and they don't bring people in. To get the word out about your church through anointed actions is to be profound.

What do people in the community think of the church? How can we turn their perception into something positive, even powerful, so that the spin works in our favor? Jesus gave us the answer when he said that the mark of a true believer would be simple acts of generosity (Matthew 25:34-46). We want the city to describe us by the simply profound things we *do*, not by our cute slogan, where we meet, or the charismatic leader we have.

CLEVER CHURCH SIGNS

Mary Katherine and David Compton collected clever invitations and admonitions they saw on church signs across the country and published their findings in a book titled *Forbidden Fruit Creates Many Jams*. Here's a sample.

God answers knee-mail

See U in S NDAY SCHOOL

Members Only: Trespassers Will Be Baptized

We aren't Dairy Queen, but our Sundays are great!

April First: National Atheist's Day

Free Trip to Heaven—Details Inside!

Where will you be spending eternity: Smoking or Nonsmoking? [1]

Building Block:
Be Anointed.

What does *anointed* mean? Sometimes people associate that word with something that is vertical—something that only God can provide mystically to certain highly spiritual individuals. On the other hand, there is a horizontal aspect to being anointed, and it has to do with the way the church is perceived by the watching world.

I have traveled around the world doing servant evangelism projects to demonstrate the kindness of Christ to people in practical ways. Because of these projects, I have heard the following words repeated hundreds of times in many languages: "I always thought that if Jesus were to come to us he would do things like this..." I've heard that thought expressed in Taiwan, Norway, the Netherlands, Germany, Mexico, Singapore, and Russia.

Anointing is both vertical and horizontal. It comes from God, but people recognize it and are drawn to us because of it. It is our secret weapon when we are building the Perfectly Imperfect Church. Anointed behavior is fun. It's natural. You don't have to write up a business plan to practice anointed behavior.

Building Block:
Be committed to small things.

Mother Teresa said she did small things with great love. I've come to believe that is the best we can do.

> *Small things done with great love will change the world.*

When our actions are anointed, we gain credibility and people listen to us. All we can do in this life is small things; at least we can do them with great love. When we try to do big things for God, we often end up doing them with small amounts of love. More often than not, we make those attempts at great things out of our own strength, not God's anointing.

Mother Teresa carried some thirty thousand people from the streets of Calcutta into her small hospice so they could die with dignity. When asked what she learned in that time, the good mother squinted her eyes and said, "I learned that I wouldn't have carried the thirty-thousandth person if I hadn't carried the first person into the hospice."

Mother Teresa gained the attention of literally the entire world—one small step at a time. It's all about putting one foot in front of the other. It's about faithfully getting up one more day, even when we don't feel much like it, and going for it one more time.

Building Block:
Be real.

People who are genuine in their behavior draw others to themselves. We need to be real. And we need tools for being real. For me the tool of choice is a toilet bowl brush. I regularly go to gas stations and restaurants and clean the restrooms to show Christ's love in a practical way. I approach the managers of the establishments and give them a big surprise by saying, "Hi, I'm here to clean your toilet." As they recover from the shock, I tell them that this is a simple and very practical way to show them the love of Christ. This is what authenticity feels like for me. Commit yourself to some authentic behavior for a while.

I also try to pray specifically to prevent my prayers from becoming inauthentic and mystical. As an exercise in authenticity, I recommend you read *The Velveteen Rabbit* by Margery Williams every night aloud for two weeks. It will do something great to your heart.

By doing a specific outreach yourself—one you don't share with anyone else—you force yourself to be in the "authentic zone." The whole "Christian zone" insulates us from authenticity. For a wake-up call, spend part of a day at your local Alcoholics Anonymous center. Don't spend all your time exclusively with believers. That gets weird.

Building Block: *Be willing to do what others will recognize as practical.*

One Sunday, as a friend of mine was enjoying a meal at a restaurant, he asked the waitress if she liked working on Sundays. She said she hated working on Sundays because church people came in on Sundays. She said they are *hard* to serve, *arrogant*, and *lousy* tippers. Her rule of thumb is that the longer they pray the less they tip!

Since that day, my friend has been on a one-man crusade to turn things around among his Christian friends. He asks, "What if Christians were *easy* to serve, *really friendly*, and always *big* tippers!" He now leaves a healthy, 20-percent tip and writes on the bottom of his credit-card receipts, "Great job! I really appreciated your service today." He reports that almost always the server will come back to the table and thank him for his nice tip and the word of encouragement. His parting wisdom: "If Christians are going to act in an unanointed way, at least they shouldn't pray before they eat to draw attention to themselves!"

Building Block:
Be willing to take a risk.

Sometimes you have to step out and take a chance that you might look silly or even stupid. That's OK—it's worth it. Jesus was "anointable" because he was always willing to do the Father's will.

Last year, Christmas Eve landed on a Sunday night. We decided to cut our services short and do an outreach to the community by giving away donuts to police, firemen, and others who had to work that night. The group I was with went to fast-food drive-through restaurants. At each one, we pulled up to the speaker to order and heard the restaurant worker's voice ask, "May I help you?"

Then I would say, "No, actually you can't. We're not here to get food. We're here to give food."

"Sir, may I help you?"

"You see, we cut church short tonight so we could all go out and give away donuts to people who have to work on Christmas Eve. We're here to give you donuts to celebrate the evening."

"Sir, please pull forward."

At each restaurant, I pulled forward to find a number of employees huddled around the drive-through window. In every case, the response was super positive; sometimes restaurant people had tears in their eyes as we drove away. The best response of the evening came at a Wendy's restaurant. After the workers cleared away and went back to work, the manager came to the window and said, "Thanks for making this an extra-special night."

"Yeah, this is a special night, being Christmas Eve and all," I said.

"No, not just that. My wife is having a baby tonight!"

"Then why are you here? Shouldn't you be with her?"

"Well, I'm pretty goal-oriented. I figured I could put in my shift here first and then meet her at the hospital. Besides, she's not that far along yet. One thing though—do you think you could pray for us tonight?"

I assured the manager that my son and I would immediately pray for him as we pulled away from the window.

I went through that drive-through a few days later, this time with a baby gift. I signed the card, "The Donut Guy," and attached my business card. A week later, the manager came to our church with his wife and brought along a few friends—fourteen in all! I think he brought all of his in-laws and the UPS guy as well. He was downright enthusiastic about coming to church.

Building Block: *Be committed to producing outward-focused disciples.*

I'm convinced that the action that most pleases the heart of God is evangelism. Some might argue that discipleship should be emphasized over evangelism, but I disagree. Our churches must develop an outward-focused people. Without a steady dose of evangelism and without new folks coming to Christ, there will not be any new disciples to worry about. What could possibly please the heart of God more than finding lost children?

One day in heaven, we will rightly describe the church by its inward activities, but that day has not yet come. Until Jesus comes again, we must push ahead in the belief that the mission of the church is all about outwardness. As we are committed to outwardness, the anointing of God will flow like a river in our midst.

Building Block: *Be amazed when God's anointing appears.*

Surprising things happen when we live in the anointing of the Spirit. Outsiders recognize what we don't even see. For example, the SoulSurvivor young people's movement in England was recognized by the Manchester police. After the group's outreach there in the summer of 2000, when eleven hundred young people did servant evangelism in the rough part of town, crime went down by 45 percent and has stayed down since that time.

Building Block:
Be willing to be near the least, the lost, and the lonely.

We have to spend time with the poor. When we are simply around the needy, genuinely looking for ways to show them God's love, God's Spirit flows through us.

Building Block:
Be willing to act in simple ways to change lives.

For years, I read Matthew 25 with fear and trembling. I saw in it an awesome warning: "You'd better watch out, you who think you are Christians. You might be a fake believer posing as a real one. You'll be exposed in the end." That warning certainly is part of the chapter's message, but there is so much more.

One day as I was reading this chapter, I experienced a paradigm shift. Matthew 25 is actually a very practical chapter that gives the church its marching orders. Verses 34-46 provide our job description, not a haunting, frightening parable.

Jesus said, "I was thirsty and you gave me something to drink."

He was saying that authentic faith always acts. A real faith doesn't just say the right words; it does the right things.

Jesus said that we would prove the authenticity of our faith to the world by doing these acts of love. As we relieve parched throats by giving drinks of water and meet the needs of the hurting by filling their stomachs with food, the people of this world will know in their hearts that we are the real thing.

Building Block:
Be willing to get away.

The combination of serving and ministering can be exhausting. You have to be able to get away for renewal. It's easy in the midst of great things going on to get caught up in the adrenaline rush of the moment and forget to take care of yourself, but an imbalance between giving and renewing will not work for long. Anointing is great stuff, but we still need to tend to ourselves and the business of balance.

ENDNOTE

1. Mary Katherine and David Compton, *Forbidden Fruit Creates Many Jams* (New York: New American Library, 2001).

Path 5: FUN!

Everything that could go south went way south that morning. It was Easter, which fell on the weekend that daylight saving time began that year, and the janitor who was to open up the building slept in until the last minute. We got into the building just a few minutes before the first of our two services. By the time we managed to get things set up just fifteen minutes late, everyone was stressed out. No one felt any emotional space for worshipping God.

All I could think of was Chevy Chase as Clark Griswold in *National Lampoon's Family Vacation*. "Are we having fun yet?" I asked. Everyone laughed and blew off some steam, and we were able to enjoy the Lord in worship.

> ***"Where the Spirit of the Lord is, there is fun!"***
> —almost 2 Corinthians 3:17

A few years ago, our church made the national news when the so-called parking-meter granny was arrested in Cincinnati for putting a dime in a stranger's parking meter so he or she wouldn't get a ticket. The people of Vineyard Community Church had been feeding parking meters for years as an act of servant evangelism, completely unaware that it was technically against a city ordinance.

When the parking-meter granny was arrested, we gained overnight prominence as the church that "illegally feeds parking meters to show God's love in a practical way." The situation was tense, to say the least. In Cincinnati it is considered bad manners to gain slightly negative national attention, so the pressure was on.

I decided to turn on the fun and flip the situation completely. First, I had T-shirts printed with a picture of our granny behind bars, and I had parking meters put on top of the bars. A caption read, "[Name Withheld], guilty of kindness" (I can't use the parking-meter granny's name in this book; she is currently in the Parking Meter Feeding Protection Program). The T-shirts made a small statement about the whole event that was clever and slightly irreverent, and they quickly became collectors' items. The shirts were the talk of the town. In fact, they made their way onto several nationally televised talk shows.

We also made fun of ourselves in a video we produced. In the video, a guy is searching his pockets for coins to feed a parking meter. A policeman approaches in slow motion with ticket book in hand. Suddenly relief comes in the form of a "kindness helicopter" that drops off a quarter. The coin comes just in time, and the policeman (a real, uniformed policeman who is a friend of ours) puts his ticket book away. Both actors wave at the helicopter. [1]

We are all trying to do something significant to glorify God. It's only natural that we should think we must be serious about our task. But it's easy to be overly serious, and that attitude can work against our efforts. It's easy to be like a Norwegian pastor and friend of mine: "Ya, we Norwegians take our joy very seriously."

Unfortunately, we diligently remove any hint of enjoyment from our task when it's involved with the church. But that joyless attitude is not the heart of God, and it's not following the model Jesus gave us. In almost every other area of life, we know how to have fun, but in the church world we fall short.

After working with people in many different contexts for more than twenty years, I have come to the conclusion that people only do something for a prolonged period of time if it's fun. That is, they quit what is not fun. We are hard-wired by God to do what is enjoyable.

Where the Spirit of the Lord is there is fun! Fun is normal—that's a given in the Perfectly Imperfect Church. A playful attitude and a church culture that allows fun can cover a multitude of shortcomings in other areas. Because of grace, we can be just who we are, just where we are in our progression of growth, and who and where we are is just fine! The discovery of that truth is incredibly liberating, though not universally understood.

For many people, the first name that comes to mind when they think of a Christian (other than Jesus) is not the Pope, Mother Teresa, or Billy Graham. It's Ned Flanders, the goofy-looking, next-door neighbor on the television show, *The Simpsons.* With his mustache, thick glasses, sweater, and irrepressibly cheerful demeanor, he is the evangelical that non-evangelicals know most intimately.

An estimated fifty million evangelical Christians live in the United States, which means that one in every five Americans is an evangelical Christian. Although heterogeneous in their beliefs, politics, and lifestyles, they recognize one another easily, and they would have no difficulty recognizing Ned and his family as their own. [2]

Ned is deeply committed to the good works of the gospel, including the random donation of a kidney and a lung to anyone who might need them. When a homeless man arrives at his front door, the family bathes him and treats his sores, gives him a new change of clothes, and sends him on his way, singing "Onward Christian Soldiers" as they work. Ned is someone

Jesus would have no trouble identifying as one of his own.

The only problem, and the reason he is the brunt of weekly jokes on *The Simpsons*, is that he doesn't have the first clue about how to have fun. The typecasting is faithful to the bitter end. Flanders is typical of modern evangelical Christians because we don't know much about fun either.

> ***"Are we having fun yet?"***
> —Clark Griswold in *National Lampoon's Family Vacation*

The Spirituality of Fun

Consider Bill, for example. A typical new attendee, Bill faces some barriers when he decides to come to church. He hasn't been the same since the divorce, and he's still getting used to the idea of the kids being with him only every other weekend. However, he's heard from several friends about a certain church. (Plus people from the same church once gave him a soda as he waited at a stoplight.)

So one Sunday morning, he dutifully pulls on his only button-down dress shirt. It's a size too small in the neck, but he figures being uncomfortable is part of going to church. It's his weekend to have the kids, so he wrestles them into church mode. They aren't exactly excited about going. By the time he arrives at the parking lot, he's pretty nervous and not much in the mood to look for God, although that's what he came to do. Still he hopes for the best.

A couple of different things could happen when Bill arrives at church. He could have a negative experience. He could feel the same as my friend's child who reported after visiting a church one Sunday, "Dad, the pastor yelled at us for an hour!" Whether he actually yelled or not, it felt like he did, and that's all that counts. Many people no doubt feel yelled at even though voices are not necessarily raised. The attitude and context make them feel that way.

On the other hand, Bill could have an entirely different experience. Imagine how Bill would feel if he arrived on the church property and was greeted by a parking attendant waving one of those large, foam pointing fingers you see at football games. Bill would probably smile and wonder, "What kind of church is this?" Imagine attendants good-naturedly pointing Bill to a parking spot then offering him a cup of coffee right there in the parking lot. Imagine that they smile—a lot.

In this picture of Bill's church experience, he meets more smiling people at the entrance of the building. As he maneuvers his kids inside, someone sees his situation and directs him to the children's area. A uniformed policeman in the vicinity of the children's area helps Bill feel secure about leaving his children with people he has never met. As he moves toward the auditorium, he is greeted once again and handed a program that explains what will be going on during the service. Another smiling face directs him to a seat and answers his questions about this new place he has entered.

After worship, a video introduces the series the pastor is doing on "Facing Life's Worst-Case Scenarios." The video is over the edge, but Bill likes it a lot. Talking to the camera, the youth leader describes having "one of those days" when everything seems to be going wrong. In the background, his car starts to roll downhill, gradually picking up speed until it hurtles into a lake and disappears under the water. [3] Although Bill doesn't know the youth leader, he laughs until he's almost crying. The crowd is still laughing and clapping as the lights come up and the pastor comes out on stage saying, "All right! Let's continue in our series on 'Surviving Life's Worst-Case Scenarios.' "

Bill is all ears. His defenses are down. When the pastor asks people to refer to their outlines, Bill is happy to oblige. He's eager to learn. He's having fun!

Each time Bill laughs, his defenses drop a little further. He returns the next week and for the next couple of months until he eventually becomes a follower of Jesus.

TOP TEN WAYS TO KNOW YOU'RE IN A BAD CHURCH:

(drum roll please)...

10. The church bus has gun racks.

9. On staff are a senior pastor, an associate pastor, and a "socio-pastor."

8. The Bible is the Dr. Seuss Version.

7. There's an ATM in the lobby.

6. Services are B.Y.O.S. ("Bring Your Own Snake").

5. Choir members wear leather robes.

4. There's no cover charge, but communion is a two-drink minimum.

3. There's karaoke worship time.

2. Ushers ask if you want smoking or nonsmoking.

And the number one way to know you're in a bad church is that the only song the church organist knows is "In-A-Gadda-Da-Vida." [4]

Defining Fun

When I use the term *fun*, I mean something different from what most Christians mean. It's not happy clappy. It's not fun as determined by children's church cutouts in Sunday school. It's not the "I've got the joy, joy, joy, joy...down in my heart" fun. It's two parts the kind of fun you could have with your little brother when you were growing up and one part David Letterman. We discovered the kind of fun I'm referring to when Dave-Steve (my associate pastor at the time) became a bit irreverent.

It's fun for fun's sake. It's saying Christian people can be fun and a little silly. This kind of fun doesn't necessarily have much to do with the message; it's just plain fun. It doesn't have much to do with anything, but that's OK.

We must give people permission to not act "spiritual" all the time. People don't have to impress anyone to be a part of the church. They can just be themselves.

VITAL FUN FACT: IT IS IMPORTANT TO HAVE PEOPLE IN LEADERSHIP THAT YOU CAN HAVE FUN WITH.

If you can be yourself and have fun with your team, your church will reflect that. If you can't, it won't. Talk with your leadership about the issue of fun. Discuss the way you want to relate to one another. You will likely have to start with small steps, but giving permission is a start.

VITAL FUN FACT: THE QUALITY OF HOSPITALITY PLAYS A HUGE ROLE IN THE FUN FACTOR.

Hospitality means a love of strangers. For example, it means making guests who have come by for dinner feel that you are thrilled that they came to your home. Hospitality is what you want to convey when people stop by your church for the first time. It's the first thing newcomers will comment on when they mention your church. Since they will evaluate how friendly you are, make their evaluations work to your benefit.

Think about what it's like to go to your church. Then think about what it's like to go to your first ballgame. When you have no idea what the seating arrangement is like, an usher to help find your seat makes all the difference in the world. Having needs anticipated and taken care of is such a relief to a newcomer.

You might also think of newcomers as if they're guests visiting your home. What do you do when people come to your house? How do you make them feel welcome? You don't sit in the living room and yell out, "Come on in." You get up and greet them warmly. You invite them into an atmosphere you've tried to make pleasant by controlling the aromas and setting the lighting so that it's just right. You don't do these things to impress your guests; you do them because you want to bring your guests into your family, to include them and make them feel comfortable.

When we do servant evangelism projects to show God's love in practical ways, from washing cars for free or distributing soft drinks to cleaning toilets, we are tacitly inviting people to church. We are saying, "God loves you," but we are also saying, "Now follow us to church." When we do that, it is our responsibility to make sure the experience newcomers have when they arrive is a positive one. In fact, their experience ought to be more than positive—it ought to be a party! My question is, "What do newcomers experience when they arrive at your church—a party or a funeral?" For the sake of our credibility, we need to have a fun environment waiting for them.

***VITAL FUN FACT:* AN ATMOSPHERE OF FUN AND ENJOYMENT CREATES A REALITY LARGER THAN LIFE.**

No explanation needed.

***VITAL FUN FACT:* THE PEOPLE UP FRONT WILL SET THE TONE FOR THE SERVICE.**

If the worship leader, the transition person, and the pastor/teacher are having fun, the people will have fun. On the other hand, people will quickly detect when a leader isn't having fun. It is imperative that all people up front have their hearts right before being "on" in public.

***VITAL FUN FACT:* AFTER WORSHIP, THE FUN FACTOR IS THE MOST CRITICAL COMPONENT OF A SERVICE.**

What you set as the priority will become the priority, and almost nothing will change your church as much as building up the fun factor will. The fun factor will permeate every aspect of your atmosphere—for the better! It's worth the effort to build fun into your mix.

***VITAL FUN FACT:* AGREE THAT IT'S OK TO POKE FUN AT EACH OTHER.**

The view of the pastor as "most highly exalted and most excellent" needs to be obliterated. It's the opposite of fun, and it's not worth propping up. It's also not an accurate view of any pastor.

> Dear Ann Landers: I am very hard of hearing, and there isn't an alarm clock in existence that will wake me up. I often set two alarm clocks, five minutes apart, and I still oversleep because I do not hear them.

Will you please tell me where I can buy a rooster? I am prepared to get a cage and follow instructions on what to feed it. I live in an apartment building in Los Angeles, and if there is a law that might prohibit me from having a pet rooster, I'd like to know about it. Thank you for your help, Ann.

S. D. in Los Angeles

Dear S.D.: If you live in an apartment building in Los Angeles and buy a rooster to wake you up in the morning, you will hear plenty—from your neighbors and the landlord, in that order. Because there are laws restricting the housing of farm animals in most urban areas, you might hear from the police as well.

Permission granted by Ann Landers and Creators Syndicate.

VITAL FUN FACT: HUMOR IS VITAL FOR LOWERING PEOPLE'S RESISTANCE.

A friend of mine likes to say, "Theology is easy; comedy is hard." What makes people laugh—hence, what makes them drop their defenses—is what we are looking for. Remember Bill, the generic newcomer? Lowering his defenses each week made it possible for Bill to find his way to Christ. The fun factor played a large role in lowering those defense barriers a bit at a time.

VITAL FUN FACT: DRESS CASUALLY.

Most people like to dress for comfort. Formal attire suggests formal, serious worship. If your church culture dictates formal attire, you're going to attract the already-Christians who enjoy an hour of serious church. A formal atmosphere is antithetical to numerical and spiritual growth.

FRIVOLITY

At least fourteen hundred college students are majoring in "golf" at eight universities, with more schools about to start such programs, according to an article by Toby Moore in The Express. One school just completed a million-dollar "learning laboratory" (a golf clubhouse). Across the country, golf courses are opening at a rate of about one a day.[5]

COMEDY VOID IN THE CHURCH?

Hoping to fill the void, The Los Angeles Times printed what it called a new line of products for the Christian practical joker in its "Off-Kilter" column. Here's a sample:

Whoopee Pews $ 129.75

When unsuspecting parishioners take their seats at church, the whoopee pew emits noises better imagined than described!

Flaming Hot Communion Wafers $ 4.95

Slip some of these into the communion dish and watch the fireworks. Looks like the real thing but makes eyes water and throat burn.

Throw-Your-Voice Talk With God Kit $ 74.99

Add life to your sermons! Increase collection revenues! Learn how to throw your voice into the choir loft, under the altar, or into collection plates. Secrets of world-famous ventriloquists revealed in 32-page booklet. Kit also includes 50-foot-high, inflatable, glow-in-the-dark Jesus.

Leaky Communion Cup $ 14.99

Looks like an ordinary communion chalice, but wine drips through tiny holes when the goblet is tipped. Especially funny when used with super-hot communion wafers.

Shock Hymnals $ 9.99

A victim who opens this book gets a powerful but harmless electrical shock. Use over and over. Never fails to catch the suckers when left around.

Flypaper Trick Bible (King James Version only) $ 12.75

The Good Book you can't put down! Just like an ordinary Bible, but the pages are made from sticky flypaper.

Surface-to-Pulpit Projectiles (set of six) $ 34.95

Pocket-sized projectiles can be launched from anywhere in church with amazing accuracy. Keep those sermons short and to the point with these tear-gas bombs. [6]

HOW TO BECOME A FUN CHURCH

- Don't do church business on Sunday morning.
- Make sure everything is ready thirty minutes before the service so you can

relax and have fun instead of feeling stressed because you were scrambling at the last minute.

- Consider using humorous video clips to augment your weekend celebrations. For a total investment of about ten thousand dollars you can purchase a video projector, a great camera, and an editing computer with software to get started in this ministry.[7]
- As a leadership group, have a heart-to-heart talk about having fun. Agree to enjoy one another. Agree to not take yourselves too seriously.
- If you are the pastor, decide to make preaching fun. Don't take yourself too seriously. Let God's joy flow through you. (If you prepare adequately during the week, you'll be much more likely to enjoy yourself when it comes time to speak.)
- Be yourself no matter what kind of personality style you are.
- Gear your humor to the crowd you have.
- Give yourself permission to have fun.

ENDNOTES

1. If you're curious, we still do servant evangelism to people in need of coins for their parking meters, but we no longer actually feed the meter. We attach the coin to the card and place the card on the car for the owner to use next time he or she needs a coin for the meter.
2. Mark I. Pinsky, "The Evangelical Next Door," Milwaukee Journal Sentinel (August 19, 2001), 01L.
3. We didn't really roll the youth pastor's car into a river. We used a junker without an engine.
4. For this and other humorous "Top-Ten" lists used during weekend celebrations at Vineyard Community Church, check out cincyvineyard.com
5. Toby Moore, "This Is America: Golf," Express Newspapers (April 13, 2001), 14.
6. Roy Rivenburg, "Off-Kilter: Churchgoers Don't Have a Prayer of Escaping These Practical Jokes," Los Angeles Times (March 17, 2000), E4.
7. If you would like to see videos we at Vineyard Community Church have done over the years, call 888.KINDNESS to order an assortment of these tapes.

Paths to the Perfectly Imperfect Church

Path 6: SAFE

After JonBenet Ramsey, Columbine, and 9/11, I don't have to tell you what kind of times we live in.

Question: If you were a pedophile where would you go on Sundays?

Answer: Probably where lots of unsupervised little kids are located.

We need to create a safe environment at every level—physical, emotional, and spiritual—if we hope to have a Perfectly Imperfect Church.

Safety is what people demand if they are going to bring their friends and family to our churches. Safety comes at many levels, starting with safe children's programs and safe facilities. Then there's the dimension of emotional safety that allows people to be real among friends and that frees them to enter wholeheartedly into community. When these lower-level safety issues are met, people are able to be "in sync" with God. Once people feel a strong sense of safety with God, they are able to take risks and hear God's voice challenge them to step into new arenas of spiritual growth.

A major role of leadership is to create environments where people can feel safe as they take experimental steps forward with God.

So What's Safe Anyway?

Feeling "safe" is feeling the *assurance that nothing is going to be forced upon a person at any time against his or her will or outside his or her comfort level.* That feeling allows people to let their guard down, be themselves, and engage in the activity at hand.

Safety was not what my church felt one Sunday evening awhile back. I'm fairly easy to distract when I'm speaking, but the circumstances of this service took the cake. Even the most focused speaker would have been distracted. As I spoke, I saw red and blue flashing lights through windows at the back of the church auditorium. A few minutes later, I saw a couple of police officers haul a disturbed-looking lady in handcuffs by the back window. Of course, I wasn't the only one who noticed all this. Keep in mind that while all of this was going on I was delivering a sermon! Later I heard more of the story.

Earlier in the day, I had met a woman who told me that she was bipolar and had been off her medication for some days. Like many bipolar people who stop taking their medications, she claimed to be feeling great, but she was not well. I told her to go home, take her medicine, and get some much-needed sleep. Instead of following my advice, she returned to our evening service. When our nursery number system called for a parent to tend to a child, she got the wild idea of kidnapping that child. In her disturbed state, she went to the nursery, claimed to be the mother of that child, and attempted to take the baby. Fortunately, we have a security system for parents picking up their kids. When she couldn't produce her security pass, the police were called, and she was arrested.

Probably the worst part of the incident was what happened in the news media. Her arrest was a matter of public record. It wasn't long until several television stations picked up on the story. In fact, it was going to be the lead story on one station's late news. We pleaded with the station and were able to convince them to put a positive spin on things. In the end, the story ran as, "Quick thinking nursery workers at Vineyard Community Church avoid catastrophe. Details at eleven." But the story could have had a far worse ending if we hadn't had a police officer on duty.

Over the years, we've been faced with many situations that challenged our church's safety zone, including people coming to church with weapons, drunk people standing up during the message to comment on my talk, Pentecostal extremists shouting out in tongues, and people shouting angry prophesies about me as the pastor. [1] Each situation has to be handled quickly and appropriately to maintain the level of safety we want people to feel.

Physical Safety

Every parent who brings a child to church needs to feel absolutely assured that the child will receive first-class treatment and that there is absolutely no cause for any concern for the child's safety. To give families this kind of assurance, we pay careful attention to details:

- We make sure that children are always with two adults and never with just one adult.
- We don't allow men to care for small children under a certain age.
- We do a background check on all children's workers to make sure they are "clean" from a police-record standpoint.

Physical safety also means designing the facility so that it promotes a sense of well-being. We have a window in every door. With the price of video monitor cameras coming down all the time, it's feasible to put a camera in each children's room and have someone watch monitors in a central room. Video tapes provide a record that can be viewed later, too. Bright lighting also gives a sense of security and safety. Children's facilities, in particular, should have bright lighting to reassure parents.

Safety and Comfort Zone

· Create a safe, fun environment for the kids. It is imperative that you inspire in parents a high level of confidence that the child care is excellent.

· Find a balance between the need to have visible security and too many people walking around with badges.

· Don't have men caring for infants. Moms will more quickly allow other moms to care for infants.

· Provide lots of light within your facility. Most churches could literally double the lighting to be where they need to be.

· Provide open spaces.

· Keep all secondary doors locked.

· Use of lots of glass.

· Put yourself in your newcomers' place. Imagine being at a Buddhist temple and not understanding anything, including the building. If you evaluate your facility from that perspective, you begin to get an accurate understanding of the way a newcomer views your place.

· Have someone in a uniform around the children's area during services. That presence says: "I'm here to make sure the kids are safe. I'm not here because there is a problem, but because we don't want a problem.

· As the leader, be sure to guard the atmosphere jealously. Are people sweltering because it's too hot? It's your job to make the building livable. Think of the five senses. How does the place smell? Professional cleanup and restoration companies can do wonders with a basement-type odor. Does the church look pleasant, or are the three folding card tables from three weeks ago still on the stage? Is the sound pleasing, or is it unbalanced? Guard the details.

TOO SAFE?

The Edmonton Journal in Alberta, Canada, reported that specially commissioned Braille posters were displayed at two locations: the University of Alberta's human resources department and the Truro Leisure Center in Truro, England. The intent was to provide equal treatment for the blind.

> **However, sighted people couldn't read the posters because the words were only in Braille, and the blind couldn't read the the limited-edition posters because they were behind glass covers for "protection." [2]**

Emotional Safety

Newcomers need to feel assured that no one is going to make them do anything they don't want to do. They need to be allowed to maintain anonymity for as long as they need that anonymity to feel comfortable. They also need to know that they will never be embarrassed at church. Never!

Emotional Safety Zone

· Be real with people. Pastors can enhance the feeling of emotional safety by disclosing their own weaknesses. But remember that the disclosures should be balanced by an ability to challenge people at the same time.

· Interpret unusual events. If you don't offer an interpretation, someone else will, and it may not be accurate. At the beginning of one of our services, a man keeled over with a gallbladder attack. There was a scene, and paramedics were called. I conveyed/interpreted to the group that the man wasn't having a heart attack, that emergency personnel were on the way. I suggested we ignore the emergency personnel as they did what they needed to do. That's what people did—they ignored the paramedics because they were informed.

· Create an environment in which one person's worship doesn't get in the way of other people's worship. I've had to talk to people who were wildly worshipping with sign language. People around them cringed and ducked, trying to avoid being hit by a flying gesture. (The worst part was that the sign-language worshippers were not hearing-impaired.)

· Allow newcomers to be anonymous. Don't smother them; give them some space. Don't ever single them out.

· Give newcomers a comfortable place to ask their questions. Give them permission to ask any questions they want to ask.

· Recognize that newcomers can be somewhat jaded. Avoid pushing them about giving too soon. Use bags rather than plates to take offerings to provide a means for anonymity.

· Provide the right amount of follow-up after a newcomer's first visit. Avoid coming across as pushy. Pay attention to the wording of the letters and communications.

· Avoid insider-only lingo. Don't say, "We're having the church picnic at Bill's farm again. It will be a great time, just like it was last year. Sally Smith will be making her good ol' apple pie once again. See you there." Avoid referring to anything that you would know but that the person walking in off the street would not know. Talk as if you have a room of neophytes who have no inkling of what you are talking about. Provide the information people might need.

You might protest: "But there aren't that many newcomers yet." Maybe so, but there won't *be* many in the weeks to come if you continue to use insider lingo.

SAFE FOR CUSTOMERS? I DON'T THINK SO.

In March of 2001, PrimeZone Media Network reported these findings about customer reactions to bad service:

- 39.3 percent complain to a store manager
- 25.7 percent tell friends about the experience and urge them not to shop there
- 22.2 percent stop shopping at that store
- 22 percent walk out without making a purchase
- 15.3 percent just ignore it
- 12.7 percent get upset but continue to shop at the store anyway [3]

Think about how these customer reactions might apply to your church.

Spiritual Safety

An atmosphere of spiritual safety begins with authentic preaching. Authentic preaching means speaking from your life lessons and often from your own pain. It isn't something you institute late in the game; do it now. This basic understanding of how spiritual safety begins will positively color all of your relationships.

GROUND RULES FOR SMALL GROUPS

- Never repeat prayer requests people have shared with you.
- Don't allow anyone to talk badly about another church.
- As the leader, protect the group from being counseled by others in the group. Don't allow "I" messages, such as "I think you should do this or that."

At the beginning of small group meetings, encourage everyone to share reasons to praise God.

Spiritual Safety Zone

· Allow people to pursue God at their own speed and at God's speed, not at your speed. From now and beyond, we need to find new ways for people to pursue faith.

· Don't try to push anyone along the journey at a faster pace than he or she is prepared to take.

There are two ways to get a chick out of an egg. One is the direct approach: Grab a hammer and use it on the egg. You'll get the chick out of the egg, but you will probably kill the chick in the process. The other approach is to put the egg in a warm, caring environment and allow the chick to come out on its own and in its own timing. The second approach is the way Jesus "incubates" new followers.

How to Increase Safety and Comfort

· Have every person representing the church wear a name tag.
· Provide police protection.
· Develop a system for picking up children and teens.
· Provide an abundance of signs.
· Assume you are dealing with unchurched strangers who have never

been to your facility—and don't know where to go.

· Include recommended area restaurants in your program. Chances are good that newcomers to your church are new to the area and don't know their way around all that well yet.

· Work on language. What do you call things? What do you call people? Do you insist that newcomers who join your church culture must add your insiders-only vocabulary to their own?

ENDNOTES

1. My favorite "prophesy" was what I call the flying-bologna prophesy. A disgruntled member said he saw me speaking with a winged hunk of bologna flying over my head. The word from God was, "Thus says the Lord, 'Steve is full of bologna!' "
2. News of the Weird (April 17, 2001), No. 688.
3. "Bad Service Drives Shoppers From Stores," PrimeZone Media Network (March 20, 2001).

Path 7: INCLUSIVE

The couple approached me with tears in their eyes.

"We've been in town for over a year, diligently checking out churches week after week. Honestly, this is the first one that has paid attention to us. We feel loved here. We were greeted four times before we made our way to our seats. Thanks for loving us."

By nature, churches move quickly into their own self-made universes. We all build exclusive cultures and keep out new people who are different. Newcomers can be changed by our message of great love, but unless the church makes an intelligent and heartfelt attempt to be inclusive, not-yet-Christians will not meet Christ's life-changing acceptance.

If you are the senior leader, your job is to connect with as many newcomers as possible. There will always be hangers-on who want to dominate your time and who have a chronic problem that needs to be tended to. But the people you need to be meeting are the people who just got there, not those who constantly need prayer for something that doesn't exist. I pray briefly for people who are in need—one or two sentences is enough. My main objective is to mingle with newcomers or anyone I don't immediately recognize.

Acceptance Versus Approval

Jesus, friend of sinners. That about says it all regarding Christ. He spent his time with prostitutes, tax collectors, and lepers. Who would he be with in today's world? He'd probably be with people who are confused about sexual issues.

> ***Jesus accepted everyone on the spot, although he didn't necessarily approve of everyone's behavior. We must do no less.***

People with certain issues are dilemmas for us. Specifically, those who have crossed the line on issues of sex present us with problems. The church doesn't know how to handle people who are attracted to people of the same sex or people who are sexually involved outside the marriage relationship. However, if we are determined to follow Jesus' example, we will reach out to people even when we can't approve of their behavior.

A few years ago, the Flynt brothers, Larry and Jimmy, came back to their hometown of Cincinnati to open a pornographic bookstore. Twenty years earlier, they had been booted out of town by the county sheriff. When the brothers became executives of the Hustler publishing empire, they desired a presence in Cincinnati. The brothers managed to maneuver around the local laws and finagle a bookstore, practically across from city hall, no less, to the embarrassment of many city officials. When the store opened, area Christians reacted. Many met the Flynts head on with protests. One flyer I received urged decent Cincinnatians to picket the establishment until the Flynts were driven out of business and out of town.

My wife and I had a different plan. We decided to be more subversive. We packed up our toilet-cleaning gear and headed out for the first of what became regular visits to the Flynts' restroom. We figured we'd show them the kindness of Christ in a profound way and invade their hearts.

The first time my wife and I went to the Flynts' store, we totally shocked Jimmy Flynt. He asked us to repeat ourselves a couple of times as though he must have misheard what we had said, but we repeated the offer. "Seriously, we just want to clean your restrooms to show you Christ's love in a practical way," we said. Finally he silently pointed to the back of the store where the toilets were located.

About a year after we started the cleaning routine (the protests hadn't succeeded in closing the store), I found myself sitting behind Jimmy Flynt on a flight from Los Angeles to Cincinnati. I didn't automatically take my seating arrangement as an invitation to talk his ear off, so I waited to see if we would bump into each other. We did exactly that on our way off the plane. I said, "Mr. Flynt, I'm Steve Sjogren."

He said, "I know who you are. You're from that toilet-cleaning church. The first time you came down to our place, I thought you were putting a bomb in our john!"

He continued, "What kind of Christians are you anyway?"

I said, "We're the kind that doesn't hate you."

As we got off the plane, we agreed to have lunch. We haven't had lunch yet; I suspect he's a bit fearful. That would be natural. I'm praying for an open door.

The distinction I make is between acceptance and approval. I was able to totally accept one of America's most notorious pornographers. I know he felt that acceptance because he stopped dead in his tracks, even with people behind him trying to leave the plane, when I said that we didn't hate him. I certainly don't approve of what he does. But if Jimmy could just give the Holy Spirit a chance to do some changing in his life, I know

God would work out the details.

If we believe God can work out the details in anyone's life, we're obligated to embrace everyone who comes through our doors.

Follow Up on Newcomers

MAKE A CONCERTED EFFORT TO GET THEIR NAMES AT WEEKEND CELEBRATIONS.

Many newcomers will be reluctant to give you their names or any other personal information during their first visit to your church. If they have visited churches before, they may expect to be hounded or called or spontaneously visited by someone from church. Any of those actions is absolutely unwanted by 99 percent of newcomers. No matter what they say at the moment, they are thinking deep down, "That's the last time I will be going to that church! It's completely unsafe."

I've heard of all sorts of approaches to making newcomers feel at home, from baking bread, pie, or chocolate chip cookies to be delivered while still warm to planting a sign in a newcomer's front yard that reads, "Thank you for visiting our church!" When I hear about such techniques, I always ask, "Is the church growing?" Almost always the answer is no. I believe that church leaders who checked would find out that all of those attempts to make newcomers feel welcome actually do quite the opposite to the majority of slightly savvy people. The direct shot right between the eyes is overkill.

Don't be dismayed that newcomers don't give you their names on their first visit. People are just that skeptical these days. I have found that it often takes three to five visits to a church before people feel enough trust to provide an address and phone number. What I say to diffuse their fears is, "If you're new, we'd love to get your name and address. We promise that we won't bug you; we'll just send you enough information to answer a few questions you might have about this church. And we'll send you an ice-cream cone in the envelope!" (I'll explain that later.)

Some churches have found they're more successful at getting people to fill out information cards if they make the cards playful. One church used a cartoon drawing of a man; it looked like a card with legs and arms and with a bit of a worried face. The card read,

Please fill this out and circle the responses that are mostly true:

1. I am here for the first time today.

2. I've been here before, and I think it's an OK place.

3. I'm getting hungry!

4. I'd like someone from the church to call me about ________________.

5. I'm wondering when this service is going to finish so I can go home!

At the bottom were spaces for the newcomer's name, phone number, and address. That card brought a very high response rate from folks. New folks enjoyed filling out the cards.

THE BIG KAHUNA PRINCIPLE

In our day, people are proud of their ability to make decisions and control their lives. Each person is the big kahuna at home, as researcher George Barna puts it. Now, I don't consider myself better or more important than anyone else. In fact, when our building crew installed a "Senior Pastor" parking spot close to our entrance, I refused to park in it. But, in fact, something powerful is communicated when the big kahuna of the church personally communicates with people visiting the church for the first time.

HAND-WRITE A NOTE ON SUNDAY NIGHT.

On Sunday night, I use a nice fountain pen or a roller-type ballpoint pen to hand-write a personalized welcome letter to each newcomer family. I know it sounds like a lot of work, but this step in the follow-up of newcomers pays huge dividends. And I disagree with those who think it's too much work. Once you get in the groove of writing notes each Sunday evening, you will find it's doable.

On any Sunday evening, I might write notes to as many as one hundred newcomers. Usually I watch a movie or two to unwind from the weekend while I write these letters. Keep in mind that the letter is not long or complicated. A typical note might say,

Dear Bob and Sally,

Glad you were with us. Hope you felt at home. Hope Bobby felt loved.

I'd love to meet you. Please come up and introduce yourselves to me after a service sometime soon.

Sincerely,

Steve Sjogren

P.S. Have some ice cream on me!

Usually people's eyes go right to a letter's postscript. In my letter, I include a coupon good for a scoop of ice cream at a good ice-cream place in town. Why ice cream? People smile when they think about eating it.

I address each envelope by hand, as well. This step is vital. When newcomers go through their mail, the first piece they will open is the most unusual one—the hand-addressed envelope. When they read the letter and realize that the pastor took the time to hand write a note and address the envelope, they will be impressed. I have been in the homes of people who've been in our church over two years and found my handwritten letter on their refrigerator. It is clear that newcomers are impressed with the effort that's involved in a handwritten note.

SEND THE LETTERS ON MONDAY.

Mailing the letters on Monday means newcomers will receive their letters on Tuesday while their visit to the church is still fresh in their minds.

CALL NEWCOMERS ON THURSDAY.

This call is strategically important. It should be very short and sweet, because it will come at a time people are not expecting it. Since the call will be intruding on their schedule, it needs to be very short—less than a minute if possible. The objective of the call is simply to take the process to the next level. When I call, I say who I am and invite the newcomers out for pie. Pie is a happy food. Everybody likes pie. It's nature's best food.

TAKE THEM OUT FOR PIE.

When I invite the newcomers out for pie (or ice cream in a pinch), I promise that we will only be about thirty minutes. During the "pie time,"

I give a brief history of the church and a micro-perspective on where we are theologically ("Billy Graham wearing blue jeans and believing in the power of the Spirit"). Then I ask if they have any questions. I don't eat much pie, as you might guess! I have found that about 80 to 90 percent of those who have pie with me end up "sticking" with the church for two years or more.

The *Process* of Inclusion

I have always been uncomfortable with models for including newcomers that are structured with stages for the newcomer to go through. You've likely seen those models. I find them unrealistic and limiting. They reflect a modern mind-set rather than a postmodern approach that is more in touch with the sorts of people who are coming into my church.

It's a good thing to have an educational track in church, perhaps a class called Church 101 to be followed by a more advanced class called Church 201, which, in turn, would be followed by Church 301 and, finally, Church 401. Our goal should be fully devoted followers of Christ. But we mustn't confuse training with true spiritual maturity. One is information-based while the latter is spiritual formation-based.

NEWCOMER'S PIZZA CLASS

We call our introductory class Newcomer's Pizza because we serve pizza to people who attend. The pizza is just an excuse to invite people. The real point of the time together is to get to know these new folks a bit and to allow them to get to know the church a bit. Specifically we want them to hear about the history of the church and about our theological "distinctives." People want to know who we are and where we are going as a church.

The distinctives that make Vineyard Community Church somewhat unique are our worship and evangelism. To illustrate both, we show a clip from the movie *Sister Act*. We show the scene that starts with the choir singing in Latin then shifting to a more upbeat version in English. In the movie, Sister Mary Clarence (Whoopi Goldberg) gets into trouble for changing the choir's style. As Sister Mary Clarence is being reamed out for the unauthorized changes, the priest and the rest of the sisters barge in. Sister Mary Lazarus, who wears a hearing aid around her neck that looks like a portable radio, perks up and says, "You know sister, there's a lot more that we could do for the people than just pray for them." The video then shows the entire convent breaking out from behind the cloister walls, cutting down the chain-link fence, and going into the community. The nuns begin to include the community in a dozen ways, and the church immediately begins to grow.

The moral behind this part of the film, and what we hope our newcomers walk away with, is that only as we break out of our cloistered lives can we begin to change the world. As we adjust our worship so that it's understandable for the average person, we will attract the attention of the watching world.

Invite people to the next step by offering other classes in addition to Newcomer's Pizza, such as "How to Get Into a Small Group" and "How to Discover Your Gifts and Talents." Be sure to offer information on where people can serve in the church. In addition, I highly recommend the Alpha course. A fifteen-session, practical introduction to the Christian faith, it is designed to help seekers find a relationship with Christ and to bring new believers into a solid relationship with Christ (see www.alphacourse.org).

Joining Vineyard Community Church

Since Vineyard Community Church doesn't have a formal membership, the concept of membership can be a little confusing and unclear. Truth be told, every church has a membership; it's just that some are formalized and some are not. We started out thinking we would not have a membership. Now that I've had adequate time to look back at the pros and cons of the issue, I wish we had gone for a formal membership. It would have clarified who was in and who wasn't. I'm not convinced that the decision to have a membership would have increased the overall commitment level, but it would have helped people qualify their relationship with the church—which would be helpful for both them and us.

In lieu of a formal membership, I developed an informal way of helping people know whether they were in or out of our ranks. If a person wants to be a part of VCC, he or she needs to:

1. **Find *God*** (Find salvation, then come faithfully on weekends and give to the cause financially.)
2. **Find a *Friend*** (Get committed to community/group relationships.)
3. **Find a *Job*** (Discover a ministry gift or talent and get involved by serving in one form or another.)

The Cycle of How We See People

Beyond the assimilation program, though, the way we see people guides everything. Acceptance allows people to be in process. Acceptance allows people to be in church even if they don't have it all together. In fact, it recognizes that no one has it all together—that we are all in process. One way to understand this constant state of process is to look at it as a cycle: from Hospital to Family to School to Army.

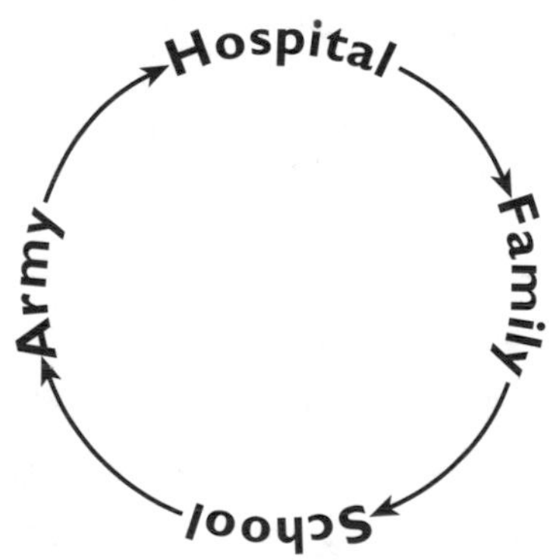

This model is different from the baseball-diamond model because it shows a person going through the cycle continuously. On the baseball diamond, a runner progresses to first base and then moves on to second base, never to return to first base. The runner moves from one base to the next to finally arrive at home plate. Theoretically a runner stays at home plate indefinitely, fully equipped to do ministry. But life doesn't work that way.

That view of humanity doesn't take into account the Jimmy Swaggart Syndrome. You're probably familiar with the sad story of his fall into immorality over a decade ago. Though his life message had been, in part, one of holiness, he was caught twice in compromising situations with prostitutes. After the first situation, he apologized on television. During that much-replayed apology, he sobbed, "I have sinned!" His sorrow was obviously very sincere. Yet not long after the dust settled on that situation, he was found with another prostitute. Later Swaggart admitted in interviews that he had quietly suffered through the shame of an addiction to pornography for decades, all the while conducting evangelistic crusades around the world.

Swaggart was stuck in a system that saw him as having arrived at maturity in Christ—at home plate. He had problems, even addictions, but his church system didn't encourage him to admit problems and ask for help.

The way life and spirituality work is more like a cycle than a straight, linear path to perfection. In my analogy there is the Hospital, the Family, the School, and the Army.

Hospital: We are all born into the hospital. We all have hurts, needs, injuries, and problems. The church needs to provide caring ministry and places where people can begin to heal, feel loved, and work on their issues. These places might include classes to help people understand boundaries, dysfunctional families, and addiction issues. Some people just need a place to rest and get re-energized after ministry burnout. When we are in the hospital, we are not yet ready to lead or serve. We shouldn't stay there forever, though; we need to cycle through the hospital.

Family: In the family, we find belonging and community, and we learn about Christ's unconditional love. As we immerse ourselves in small groups, we experience forgiveness and acceptance, and we learn to love without condition.

School: School trains us and equips us for life and ministry. This is where we develop our skills and become more effective.

Army: The powers of darkness cringe at the awesome power of the light of the church as it is represented in fullness in the army of God. In the army, we do the work of the church: intercessory prayer, serving, leading, and helping. But as we serve in the army, we can be wounded by the warfare.

Here's how the progression works. As we move naturally from the hospital, or the caring ministries of the church, we become part of the family. The family embraces us in an atmosphere of acceptance and forgiveness, which prepares us for school. At school we learn about the unique ministries that God has given us. Once we are adequately equipped, we enter the army, where exciting ministry and warfare take place. But once we're in the army, it probably won't be long before we're wounded. Wounds wear us down until, eventually, we're unable to work effectively in the army of God, and we become dysfunctional.

That's when we have a need to return to the hospital for a visit to repair ourselves. Sometimes work in the army uncovers things from the past, and we need to work on them. Whatever the problem, people should feel safe enough to admit that they need the healing of the hospital from time to time. When the hospital has done its healing work, it's a good idea to delve more deeply into the family of small groups and then to receive more training in school to avoid again making the ministry mistakes that put us in the hospital.

HOW TO BE MORE INCLUSIVE

- Redefine *evangelism* to mean "bringing and including."
- Establish a process for bringing newcomers into the life of your church, and diligently follow up on those new people God brings your direction.
- Develop a winsome system for greeting and ushering.
- Observe the spiritual progress of those God is bringing you.
- Talk about inclusion with your team again and again and again—until that's all they sell. The success or failure of what we do rides on our ability to include newcomers in what we are doing. Without an inclusion mentality, we are sunk.
- Find an Inclusion Cheerleader other than the senior leader. Typically a good candidate for the Inclusion Cheerleader will be an older person who is

financially stable so that he or she will have the time to do the job. This person won't have a theological axe to grind. In our church, his name is Ron. Perhaps you have a Ron in your church just waiting to be identified. Give this book to the Ron in your church who wants to make newcomers feel warm and included. Ron can make others successful and can coach people in the church about how to be inclusive. Ron has the patience and heart and time to do the job.

Path 8: TRUSTING

"Oh the inexpressible comfort of feeling safe with a person; having neither to weigh thoughts nor to measure words, but to pour them all out, just as they are, chaff and grain together, knowing that a faithful hand will take and sift them, keep what is worth keeping, and then, with the breath of kindness, blow the rest away."

—George Eliot

It was a snowy night. When it snows in Cincinnati, people freak out. Just a little of the white stuff causes them to stay indoors for the day. I wondered if I should cancel our small-group meeting that night, but decided we'd be like the mail delivery: Neither rain, nor sleet, nor snow would keep us from meeting.

Our group of about a dozen people was about half that size that evening. My first impression was that it was going to be a slow night. It's difficult enough to get people to open up and share in a small group, much more so when the group is only six people.

But that night the subgroup of the small group bonded in a peculiar way. We experienced some of the community that the Scriptures promise will happen when we gather as believers. Maybe we felt bonded because we had all braved the storm to be together, but we shared deeply that night. People opened up and shared dreams about the future. Some shared their fears about what might kill those dreams.

As we finished up that night, one woman shared, "You know, this is as close to 'family' as I've ever had in my life. Thanks." With hearts full of encouragement, people ventured out to brush off cars that had several more inches of snow piled on them and slowly made their way home. They all checked in when they made it home. Amazingly no one got stuck in the snow.

> ***"Before we can be greatly used by God, we must see the monstrous evil in our souls."***
> —David Roper

It's been a few years since that snowy night, but it remains as clear as ever in my mind's eye. I think I will forever keep that inclement-weather night in my heart. What happened that night demonstrated part of the reason I became a Christian—the hope that I, a dysfunctional person struggling through life, could find other dysfunctional people and that somehow, by the power of God, we could learn to get along. It's the hope that God has placed in my heart to know and experience the kingdom of God here on earth. When it happens, it is evidence that God is at work, because none of us can create that experience on our own, apart from God.

> ***"Sin is my nature, the only thing I know how to do."***
> —Brother Lawrence

To know and experience God's kingdom here on earth, we need to trust one another. By *trust*, I mean the willingness to come into community—to trust others enough to open our lives up to one another. Small groups aren't the only way to develop that kind of community, but they are the easiest and most direct method I know of.

Churches will never grow past a weekend attendance of two hundred people until they get small—until they get into community through small groups. There is no better way to develop leaders. There is no better way to develop disciples who will understand and embrace the values of the Perfectly Imperfect Church than through the development of small-group leaders and small groups. [1]

> ***"A person's a person, no matter how small!"***
> —the philosopher Horton the Elephant

Like a Big Small Group

If your church has a weekend attendance of fewer than two hundred people, the first thing you need to do to get small and create community is to go to two services. That move will develop the need for small groups. Small groups won't work unless you have two services because your weekend service will serve as your small group.

I suggest having two services your first week together as a church. I coach all of my church planters to provide two services the first week of offering Sunday services, no matter how small the church is. Two services will break up the "we four and no more" clique mentality that is so common in small churches.

It is almost impossible to have a successful small-group ministry with only one service because everyone is already seeing everyone, especially in the small church. Once a group grows to more than thirty people, it is impossible to know everyone at a level deeper than merely knowing names. But people won't feel the need to gather in smaller groups until the group has divided into at least two smaller subsets.

If a small group is to survive, it must have some sort of outreach component. The fastest way to kill a small group is to make it an inwardly focused entity. I have seen many groups die from infighting over miniscule issues that likely could have been taken care of if there had simply been an outward element to the group.

I recommend that each small group define what a normal outreach schedule in their calendar of meetings should be. For example, if the group meets every week, planning outreach for every sixth meeting might be reasonable. The outreach projects should be simple and close to where the group meets. (See my book *101 Ways to Reach Your Community* for outreach-project ideas). Begin the outreach meeting together to talk briefly about what the outreach will be. Then go out for an hour to do the project. After the outreach project, bring the group together again to discuss how things went and have some refreshments.

It is imperative that the senior leadership be involved in authentic relationships if the people of the church are to get involved as well. As the leaders do, so do the people. Too often I have seen senior leaders aspire to get the people in their congregations involved in small groups without actually being heartily involved in small groups themselves. There's no credibility in that leadership, and the encouragements to get involved fall on deaf ears. Let your enthusiasm flow out of your own involvement and experience.

FEELING KIND OF KIND—FAKE COMMUNITY

MDMA's ("Ecstasy") effect on the brain is to hyperstimulate the manufacture of serotonin. The torrent that is unleashed brings about a state of consciousness in which it is difficult to feel anxious or depressed, or anything other than love and warmth and good will toward oneself and one's fellow human beings. [2]

How to Have a Great Small-Group Meeting

START ON TIME.

Reward the people who are on time by starting on time. Don't punish them by waiting for latecomers to show. Waiting for latecomers rewards and reinforces tardy behavior.

OPEN WITH A PREVIEW.

Say, "I'm glad you're here!" and explain what will happen. For example, you might say, "We'll worship with two or three songs. Then we'll share the good things God has been doing in our lives. Then we'll look at the Bible for a bit. At the end, you'll have time to share your prayer requests."

WORSHIP.

Worship is optional. Sing if your group enjoys it.

SHARE GROUND RULES.

- Keep what's shared confidential.
- No counseling of other group members.
- No complaining about other churches.
- The meeting will be done within one and a half to two hours. If you want to hang out for a little bit, you can. But you are free to leave at that point.

DO SOME GET-TO-KNOW-YOU STUFF.

The leader should have a vision for the group that includes helping people get to know each other. The classic activity is to have people introduce themselves and tell a little about themselves. The Serendipity Bible offers hundreds of open, safe questions that can help people begin to share and get to know one another. Another twist is to have people pair up to talk and then have each person share with the group what the other person said.

SHARE.

Invite people to share something good that God has been doing in their lives. Remind people to save prayer requests and needs for later. If people begin to become negative, take charge by saying, "We'll share our prayer needs later in the meeting. This is the time we share the good things the Lord is doing in our lives."

DO YOUR STUDY.

Keep the study part simple so that studies can be used again as the groups reproduce. Use good discussion questions and don't preach. Don't let anyone dominate the response time with a too-long response. Keep the study time interesting by encouraging a lot of people to contribute. It's fine to call upon people who aren't contributing by name and ask what they think of the question at hand. Some people will not share unless they are called upon.

PRAY.

Vary how the prayer time is done, but make it a time to bring up needs. One option is to stay together and pray as a group as long as the prayers are kept short. One-sentence prayers are great. Another option is to break into groups of three so people can pray for one another in the groups. One person in each group should be appointed the leader. The second option takes a little longer, so more time needs to be allotted for it.

If people pray in groups of three, remind everyone that it is a *prayer* time, not a counseling time.

HAVE REFRESHMENTS.

Refreshments aren't essential, but something simple will encourage people to gather at the end of the meeting to talk and get to know each other. So that providing refreshments doesn't become a burden on the host, encourage people to take turns bringing the refreshments.

The Makeup of a Small Group

GROUP LEADER

The group needs a leader to pull the group together and keep things going.

APPRENTICE LEADER

The apprentice may be the most important member of the group because he or she will take the next group as the original group multiplies—something that should happen sooner rather than later.

HOST AND HOSTESS

The host and hostess open their home to the group and create an environment that is warm and inviting for all. With good hosting, a group will thrive. Without it, it will not grow. The home you choose for your meetings should be easy to find. I've been in groups that met in homes that were great *once you got there*, but the homes were almost impossible to find and therefore not the best choice. Also consider parking, the noise level in the home, and any other distractions. Where child care is a concern, consider hiring a reliable neighbor to watch children in her home. Teenagers you know and trust can also be good choices for child care, but the children should not be in the home where the meeting is held.

WORSHIP LEADER

I see worship as an option, but it is a great addition if you can do it well. Small-group worship almost has to be done with guitar accompaniment, considering the limitations of mobility and people's skills (it's difficult to sing and play the trombone at the same time!). Worship should be short and sweet—no more than fifteen minutes if you are keeping to the ninety-minute to two-hour schedule.

OUTREACH LEADER

The outreach leader is a cheerleader who keeps the group looking outward. Not all of your outreaches will go smoothly or seem successful, so the outreach leader should be someone with an indomitable spirit that keeps on keeping on in spite of the odds. This person also needs to be creative and able to work with little to make much because there will be less-than-ideal situations as you prepare to go out to do outreach.

How to Reproduce Small Groups En Masse ("Turbo-Groups")

Think about small-group expansion and reproduction as soon as you begin to form your small-group system. To prepare for expansion, I've developed turbo-groups to train several group leaders at once in a relatively short time. Over the years, I have had great success using turbo-groups to train lots of small-group leaders.

I train leaders and then place their names in a "ready-to-go" pool. These potential leaders are told upfront that they will not necessarily be given a group to lead upon the completion of the training period. I allow practically anyone who has a desire to be trained to take the small-group training. I offer the training based on the let-the-cream-rise-to-the-top principle. Those who are the best budding small-group leaders will be apparent by the end of the training period.

> *"You can easily judge the character of others by how they treat those who can do nothing for them or to them."*
> —Malcolm Forbes

The most profound movie I've viewed in the past few years is *Freaks*, a 1932 film starring circus sideshow folk. In today's politically correct vernacular, we would call them special-needs people. The characters in this film have astounding physical disabilities. Some are hard to believe even when you see them. (The film was banned in England for decades because the physical disabilities it shows are so disturbing.)

The movie has had such an impact on me that I'm a bit of a *Freaks* salesman; I'll show it to anyone who expresses the least bit of interest in its message. Though the self-named freaks face incredible difficulties on a daily basis, none of them chooses to sink into self-pity for a minute. (Without ruining the story for you, it's the "normal" people who are the real "freaks," as it turns out.) These sideshow folks find great joy and satisfaction in simple lives lived in authentic community. Their basic needs are met as they do what they love, which is working together in the circus. They get through life and are fulfilled because, more than anything else, they have one another. The film presents a compelling picture of a trusting community—a picture that I think is close to the imprint for belonging that God has placed in all our hearts.

> ***"When you stand at the Pearly Gates, would you rather be told that you were too forgiving or you were too judgmental?"***
> —Leonard Sweet

ENDNOTES

1. When I use the term small group, I'm talking about the entire range of community-building mechanisms. I believe that traditional small groups, as they are typically understood, do not work well with certain age groups—Generation X people, for example, who typically prefer to not meet in homes in small numbers. In some ways, the way we think

of small groups is more of a baby boomer idea. It is the best mechanism we have at hand now, but the bottom line is that we need to learn new ways of developing authentic community, in whatever form it takes.

2. Gary Greenberg, "Doctor X," Rolling Stone (April 26, 2001).

Path 9: ATMOSPHERIC

I recently visited two cathedrals that represented vastly different theological perspectives. One was the historic national cathedral on Mexico City's city square. The building is so old that it's beginning to tilt and sink into the lake bed it was built on hundreds of years ago.

I walked in during a Saturday night mass and saw a sanctuary filled with the soft light from hundreds of candles that had been lit by the worshippers. With my limited Spanish, I understood about every tenth word, and I heard frequent references to Maria. During my thirty-minute stay, I observed how people sang their way through the Roman Catholic mass with great gusto. It was clear that these people loved God the Father and his Son, Jesus. While I seriously disagree with much of the theological content of the Roman Catholic message, I believe Catholics are brothers and sisters in Christ (they believe more than I do, not less). I felt the presence of the Holy Spirit at that service.

Contrast that scene with another cathedral I visited in Bern, Switzerland. This historic site was at the center of several Reformation events. The word of God has been faithfully proclaimed there and continues to be to this day. While these Reformed people may be technicians of God's Word, I'm sure they don't realize the vibes they give off. My experience there was absolutely antithetical to the love and warmth I find in the grace of Christ. From the brusque tour guides who unemotionally explained the history of the building in hushed tones to the chilly room temperature, the entire experience would have been a turnoff to any not-yet-Christian contemplating the possibility of following Christ. I dare say the people at that cathedral may possibly be doing more damage than good to the cause of Christ.

No doubt as some of you are reading these sentences, a verse from Isaiah is flashing through your minds: "My word...will not return to me empty, but will accomplish what I desire" (Isaiah 55:11). Yes, that's true. Praise God that's true because, in light of the often pathetic job the church has done in creating an atmosphere that is conducive to attracting outsiders, we might otherwise have no fruit whatsoever. We can do much better!

Those two places of worship are studies in atmospheric contrasts: One having a not-so-accurate belief system but a great atmosphere; the other, very precise and unquestionably biblical beliefs but a deadly atmosphere. We don't have to choose between those two extremes; we can have right beliefs and a fantastic atmosphere that is conducive to embracing those beliefs.

One of our servant evangelism projects is to give away Popsicles. Our church has its own Popsicle truck, complete with children's music. It's just like the ice-cream trucks you grew up with. Equipped with special hydraulics, which allow it to bounce when it's driven, our truck draws a crowd wherever it is parked. We create an atmosphere that's larger than the mere elements of the truck and the treats it contains. The ice-cream truck builds a presence. Its atmosphere is complete with sights, sounds, and tastes.

We recently stole the show at a local parade by driving the truck at the end of the parade, just after a battalion of motorcyclists in full regalia. The truck bounced along, playing its music and distributing thousands of Popsicles to hot parade-goers.

Atmosphere Architects

We are all called to be atmosphere architects in God's kingdom. The senior leader is to be the prime architect. His or her job includes oversight of the celebration experience, as well as leading people to experiences in generosity, outreach, and community. With a watchful eye, the architect applies the glue that holds the atmosphere together.

We were sponsoring a "Free, No Kidding Car Wash" one Saturday. I was serving as the atmosphere architect that morning, tending to all the details that go into making a car wash a party and not a funeral. I've learned that the best cars are the last cars of the day. Today was no exception. A woman pulled in near the end of a day, and as she got out of her car, I had a sense that she was burdened emotionally. As her car was being tended to, I asked if she had any prayer needs. As is typical when I ask that question, she said she was doing just fine. So I rephrased my question. I asked, "If Jesus were standing here right now, what would you ask him to do for you?"

She said, "Oh, that's different. I'd ask him to free me from my grief. You see, my grandma, who I was very close to, died a week ago today. In fact, I've been thinking about her all day today. I miss her terribly." I asked if she would mind if I prayed for her, and she said she would appreciate it. Judging by her response, I suspect she pictured me praying at the end of the day, with a prayer something like, "Now I lay me down to sleep...and God bless that lady at the car wash." But I meant I would pray for her right on the spot. And I did.

Often when people are served, they respond to things in an emotional way, so over the years I've come up with a *tear-meter*, an emotional-response rating system. It runs from one to ten. A one on the scale is the manly tear that brims in the eye but doesn't quite trickle down the cheek. I have found that only men are capable of such tears. When women cry, they jump right into a higher level on the scale. A level-three tear trickles part way down the cheek but evaporates before it hits the chin. Level five tears actually drip off the chin on both sides of the face. At level seven, both the tears and the nose are engaged at the same time. You might wonder if there is actually a level ten on this scale. There is, though I've only seen it a couple of times. At level ten, a person is so worked up the tears actually jump off his or her face horizontally instead of dropping vertically. It's quite a sight.

As I began to pray for the woman at the car wash and ask the Holy Spirit to relieve some of her pain, she began to cry profusely. She went right into level seven tears. It was beautiful. The Lord touched her when she was least expecting it. The best part was that it happened outdoors at a busy gas station. Though the external atmosphere was far from ideal, God created a just-right spiritual environment that worked fine.

All churches create an atmosphere. *Atmosphere*, as used here, is what people feel in a church. It's not the left-brain, linear programs. It's not the things that are seen but the unseen. Those unseen intangibles are speaking volumes to your attendees and are especially noticeable to newcomers.

Tuning your attention to the atmosphere means learning to notice things you wouldn't normally notice. Many elements make up the atmosphere at the mall. However, because you have been to the mall many times, you take that environment for granted. If those elements—as subtle as they are—were missing, you would notice that the mall just wasn't the same.

In the same way, we need to attune ourselves to building and maintaining a warm and inviting atmosphere that works with our vision for what church should be.

GOD'S KINGDOM IS AN ATMOSPHERE

Craig Van Gelder wrote that the kingdom of God isn't a place as much as it is what I call an atmosphere. According to Van Gelder, "The basic idea of the kingdom is that God in Jesus powerfully entered human history with a reign that re-established life on the basis of redemptive power." The

kingdom of God, he said, is about the "dynamic presence of God's redemptive power confronting the forces of evil and restoring life to its fullness." [1]

Fine Tuning the Atmosphere

Consider some of these adjustments to the atmosphere that you are creating in your church.

ATMOSPHERE ADJUSTMENT: COFFEE IN THE SANCTUARY

I know, some of you are gasping for breath right now. "Coffee in the sanctuary! That would never fly at our church." I had that same reaction when this idea first surfaced, but there is nothing more powerful in changing the atmosphere of your church than to allow coffee (with lids!) into your sanctuary. Some would say, "But what about the carpet. We'll soil it." Coffee is a community building drink. No matter what possible mess is created (we've allowed coffee for years and have had very few accidents), it's well worth the trouble for the atmosphere that is created.

ATMOSPHERIC ADJUSTMENT: LIGHTING

Stage lighting is vital for the creation of a great atmosphere. Lights are an investment upfront, but they are well worth it when installed and controlled properly with gel filters. There are only a few things that can be totally controlled in the auditorium environment. The lights are one of them.

For the congregation, we have found that softer lighting during worship works well. We increase the lighting as needed for people to take notes or read from their programs.

ATMOSPHERE ADJUSTMENT: COLOR

If you have inherited a vintage building, you probably have some interesting color schemes to work with. For the most part even a horrendous color problem can be solved with new carpeting and a coat of paint. Empower your "design team" to submit a few color schemes to keep your environment fresh and inviting. Think of the paradigm, "inviting family room," not "formal living room." For ideas, look at a few newer hotel lobbies, where designers created an atmosphere that makes people want to come and stay.

Keep in mind, you communicate value to the people coming as you take the time and energy to create a truly welcoming space for them.

ATMOSPHERE ADJUSTMENT: PACE AND FLOW

Is there a sense of nervousness to your services or a relaxed flow to things? Adjust your transitions to make your service flow comfortably. The way you come across has everything to do with how you communicate internally with your team.

ATMOSPHERE ADJUSTMENT: BEFORE AND AFTER

Just as Musak is played at the mall to create an atmosphere, we play worship music as people are entering and leaving our facility. It puts people who are coming in into a mode of worship. Many walking in to the facility are not doing well emotionally; they need all the encouragement they can get.

ATMOSPHERE ADJUSTMENT: STAGE APPEARANCE

Your people have to look at the front of your stage for at least an hour each weekend. They will notice little things, daydream, and count the bricks, but hopefully pay attention to the excellent teaching. What does your stage say?

Is your stage cluttered? Are cords strewn all over? Is the overall look inviting or chaotic? Are your people on stage like the rest of the people who attend the church or do they wear special clothing that sets them apart (a negative in my mind). Women should be conscious of their clothing, that is, not too tight and not too short, as a stage is usually set higher than the congregation. Provide a full-length mirror backstage so musicians, singers, and speakers can make sure everything is in order.

ATMOSPHERE ADJUSTMENT: MINIMIZE DISTRACTIONS

Empower your ushers (hosts, greeters, elders, helpers—whatever you call them) to help minimize distractions from any source. Babies in the congregation can be a major distraction, for example. The mother is sometimes oblivious to the sounds that her child is constantly making. She has grown accustomed to a certain noise level and is thrilled to be out of the house. Another mom may be mortified that her child is noisy but be frozen in her seat to avoid creating a further scene by leaving.

In either case, the usher can politely ask, "Would you mind standing in the back? The baby is distracting others from hearing the message." (I have found that a female usher making that request is better received than a male.) A cry room, TV monitors in the hallways, sugarless suckers, crayons, and coloring sheets are all possible helps to the situations. Although you risk offending a mother and her "perfect child," you are sure to offend many by doing nothing.

ATMOSPHERE ADJUSTMENT: TEMPERATURE

Is it too warm or too cold? Usually the problem is that it's too warm. It's difficult to pay attention to the message when it's difficult to stay awake.

ATMOSPHERE ADJUSTMENT: SEATING

This is the third element that can be controlled, in addition to lighting and temperature. Is your seating comfortable? Is it easy to get to? If you have flexible seating is the spacing adequate so that you aren't frustrating people?

HOW TO BUILD ATMOSPHERE

- Good atmosphere means saying no to certain things. Say yes to the things that will allow that atmosphere to flourish. Say no to what will impede that vision from being realized.
- Analyze your services. Consider hiring "secret shoppers": pay $30 to individuals who come and give their honest opinion about what they experience. You need the details about the atmosphere that they can offer you.
- Surround yourself with the right people. They can greatly affect atmosphere.
- Pay attention to who's answering the phone at your church. Are they

conveying the atmosphere you want them to? Are they part of the solution, or are they furthering the problem? By the way, did you know that people can hear a smile over the phone?

- Allow room for mistakes. Don't demand that people upfront be perfect.
- Be bold! Remember you're leading a movement. Expect change, and help your people to expect it.
- Atmosphere is greater than the sum of its parts. Therefore, atmosphere is worth guarding. It's holy. It's what makes this thing go forward. It's the nuclear powered engine of all that you are doing.
- Conduct weekly staff meetings as though you were already a Perfectly Imperfect Church in size and focus. Reiterate the dream and vision.
- Build expectation. Anticipate that when you get together something great is going to happen. Remember that anything is possible when God shows up.
- Begin now to create the atmosphere you want to see in the future, and make it happen.
- Don't get overstressed about details and miss the big picture of what God is doing in your midst. It's possible to go overboard on making every single aspect of your services neatly fit into your airtight view of how a celebration ought to go.

ENDNOTE

1. Craig Van Gelder, *The Essence of the Church* (Grand Rapids, MI: Baker Books, 2000), 75.

PATHS TO THE PERFECTLY IMPERFECT CHURCH

Path 10: GENEROUS

The night of the event, the place was buzzing. The room was jam-packed, with standing room only. There were so many people that I felt a little claustrophobic.

Let me backtrack a little. Vineyard Community Church was about to move into a new, multimillion-dollar facility, but we still needed several hundred thousand dollars for our real estate deal to go through. We had planned on using the money from the sale of our old facility to help finance the new one—until we felt that the Lord was showing us we should do something completely counter to logic.

We had tried to sell the building for several months but had found no serious interest. As we prayed about the situation, we began to feel that the reason the building wasn't selling was that we were not to sell the building. We came to believe that we were to give the building away. God confirmed to me and to others that we were to give the church to a growing African-American church that was very interested but couldn't afford it. It didn't make sense logically. We were struggling ourselves to come up with enough money to get into our new facility. What were we thinking with this crazy idea of giving away a building that was worth a million dollars? To top it off, we didn't fully own the building we wanted to give away! Though we had been in that facility for a number of years, we had never made it a priority to pay it off. We owed about $850,000.

I shared with our congregation the idea of giving away the building, and people went wild with excitement! We all agreed to keep it a secret from the other church while we all gave sacrificially for the next six weeks. We agreed to have a joint baptism service with the other church at the end of six weeks to spring the surprise on them.

The money came in by spurts, and it came in amazing forms. People sold things that were meaningful to them to raise the cash we needed. Children made art and sold it. People sold their vacation homes. One woman sold the Barbie doll collection she'd kept since childhood. We received motorcycles, cars, boats, and RVs.

A few days before the big night, we were still more than $100,000 short of our goal of $850,000. It seemed that people had given all they could give. So a few days before the due date, several of the pastors and I decided to hold a vigil. We announced that we would be at the church for twenty-four hours straight and that if people wanted to stop by and either pray or give money they were welcome. What happened was amazing. There was a steady flow of people throughout that twenty-four hours. Some people dropped off more materials they wanted to donate. People dropped off lots of checks. Some stopped by to sit in the auditorium in stillness in the middle of the night.

One of the last to stop by was a little boy on his way to school. His mother dropped him off, and in he walked with a bank full of change. He said he had been saving it to give to Jesus. When we tallied it all up—including what the little boy gave at the last minute—the total was just more than $850,000.

When the big night arrived, we printed up a 2x4-foot check for the gift amount. The church receiving the check was completely surprised. Some of the choir people actually fainted when the announcement was made! People in our church felt such an adrenaline rush that later many told me they couldn't sleep that night. When everything was said and done, when the lights were turned off and the last cars drove out of the parking lot, I was the last to leave. The building was no longer ours—and it felt great.

A Theology of Generosity

After experimenting with the power of generosity for the past few years, I have come up with a theology of generosity. I don't recall ever seeing such a theology in print before. It's not complicated, but it is biblical and it works.

GENEROSITY IS UNCANNY.

As a friend puts it, "Our commitment to generosity has to be freaky!" Generosity isn't something you can dabble in; it's a lifestyle to be embraced. There's no middle of the road. You're a person who embraces generosity, or you're a person who doesn't. Generosity comes from the work of the Holy Spirit in our lives. It's better caught than taught.

GENEROSITY IS LARGER THAN LIFE.

Generosity is larger than the key concept of outreach, and it is bigger than the matter of fun. It's the most important of all the concepts of the Perfectly Imperfect Church. It's the fountainhead of it all when it comes to having a heart for God's kingdom.

GENEROSITY IS CONTAGIOUS.

When one or two people hop onboard with the practice of generosity, more are sure to catch the raw excitement. When we gave our building away, not everyone was thrilled with the idea at first. After a few weeks, though, it was impossible to not be stoked about the project. People later told me they became impulse givers (similar to impulse shoppers but in a positive sense) because they were swept up in the excitement of it all.

GENEROSITY COMPELS US TO GIVE TO THOSE WHO ARE DIFFERENT FROM US.

The natural inclination is to give to people who are like us. We want to give only to those who are "worthy" or who "think right." But the power of generosity compels us to reach out beyond the comfort of our own lives and into the lives of those who are different from us. The church we gave our facility to was a black congregation. Cincinnati is a fairly segregated city, so the idea of giving to this group was no doubt a stretch for some people. But by the end, giving to that congregation was an overwhelming joy. We remain closely affiliated with that congregation today.

GENEROSITY IS AN ADVENTURE.

Generosity is an adventure like no other. We sow seeds, and we wait to see what will grow. We do our part, and we trust God to bring fruit in his timing. It's energizing to see what God will do!

GENEROSITY IS THE NORM IN A KINGDOM THAT SEEMS BACKWARD AND UPSIDE-DOWN TO THE WORLD.

We are really right side up, but giving away freely seems ludicrous to those who are not in the kingdom of God.

WHAT CAN *YOU* DO TODAY?

In an editorial piece written for Newsweek magazine, Jack McConnell described gathering around the dining-room table with his brothers and sisters. At every meal, his father, a Methodist minister, would ask each of the seven children, "And what did you do for someone today?"

Many years later, McConnell remembered his father's question. After a successful career in medical research, he and his wife retired to a home on Hilton Head Island, South Carolina. The home was in a gated community amid yacht clubs and golf courses. Beyond the gated community, though, native islanders lived a very different existence. Among the necessities of life these gardeners, maids, and construction workers did without was medical care.

McConnell decided to do something for someone. With the help of other retired doctors on the island, he started a clinic to provide free primary health care to people in need of it. He convinced the state legislature to come up with a special license for volunteer doctors in not-for-profit clinics and found reasonable malpractice insurance. The town donated the land, and residents donated supplies. In 1994 the clinic opened. It logged five thousand patient visits that year. In 2000, the clinic saw sixteen thousand patient visits. And by then, other Volunteers in Medicine (VIM) clinics were opening around the country, all staffed by those who understand that it is better to give than to receive.[1]

Generating Generosity

Our churches need to be known for generosity outside the church walls, as well as inside them. Christian generosity has typically been aimed at others within the church walls. We must export our generosity in big, audacious ways that will grab the imagination of the people around us. When outsiders think of us, what should automatically come to mind are people freely giving of their money, energy, and gifts to make our cities and towns better places. Our goal is to cause people to smile when they hear about the latest venture, our most recent sacrificial hit of generosity. We need to have people think, "These guys really go the extra mile, don't they."

All we need to get started are some good ideas. The following are some "Generosity Generators" to get you going. I recommend that, as you read these, you write your own ideas in the margin as they come to you.

Generosity Generator: *As a church body, start with percentage giving.*

Begin to grow in generosity by disciplining yourself to designate a certain percentage of your church's budget to be given others. I recommend starting by dedicating 3 to 5 percent of your budget to local outreach. However, the main thing is to *start with something* set aside for generous outreach efforts.

You've probably heard the term, "Tithes and *offerings*" as in, "Let's take up our tithes and offerings" during a weekend service. The "offerings" part of that phrase refers to giving beyond what a person normally gives to the local church. I recommend that you start a special offering fund and use it only for special financial needs that others in your community will have.

Generosity Generator: *Every so often, be outlandishly generous.*

Vineyard Community Church has been sending teams to Mexico City's dumps to minister to the people who make their living recycling what they find there. These people have many medical needs. Our teams spend about ten days at a time ministering to these folks. The trips cost about a thousand dollars per person. One weekend, as I encouraged people to give this mission a try, I offered to personally pay the first one hundred dollars if anyone needed help with raising the money for the trip. It was a spontaneous idea; I probably should have asked my wife before I made the offer! But then, I didn't expect thirty-two people to take me up on it! Janie understands about my spontaneous ideas and took this one in stride. To my surprise, some thirty-five people came forward during the following week, without any prompting, and gave a hundred dollars each toward the project!

Remember that in the theology of generosity that generosity is a sport. Every once in a while we need to do something outlandish.

My friend, Pastor Denny Bellesi at Coast Hills Community Church in Orange County, California, came up with an amazing idea. He called one hundred random people in the congregation to come forward and gave each of them a $100 bill to invest in the community during a ninety-day period. His idea was to encourage them to find creative ways to live out the parable of the talents. Once the church's money was handed out, the creativity started to flow. One of the $100-bill recipients told his men's group about the project, and by the end of the meeting, that single bill had turned into $2,300 for outreach funds. Another man invited four friends to dinner: a Christian, a Jew, a Buddhist, and an agnostic. He divided the $100 among them. The Christian and the agnostic teamed up and raised $1,500 to send children with cancer to camp. The Buddhist bought coats, gloves, and hats for homeless people. The Jewish woman raised another $50 and bought $75 worth of McDonald's hamburgers for a homeless shelter. When the manager heard about the project, she threw in hot apple pies.

At last count the original $10,000 has turned into $150,000. A small investment with a fabulous return. That's the business we're in!

Generosity Generator: *Start a twenty-dollar giveaway challenge.*

Challenge people to see what they can do with twenty dollars in one week. Whether the church provides the money or people provide their own start-up money, the idea is to challenge people to use that money in a generous outreach idea that will touch as many people as possible. Give general instructions, including, be wise, be legal, and be a servant in whatever you do. At the end of the week, gather the stories and share them the following weekend to build up your church and spread the excitement about generosity.

Generosity Generator: *Practice generosity by tipping well.*

As I mentioned earlier, we need to change the perception restaurant workers have of Christians. Each time we eat out we participate in a lab experiment—a chance to grow in generosity.

Typically customers who don't drink alcohol don't tip as well as customers who do drink alcohol. When I don't order an alcoholic drink, the servers look a little downcast. I often ask, "So, what's your best tip of the day?" I tell them, "I may drink iced tea, but I tip like Jimmy Buffet."

TIPPING THE SCALES

A church in Charleston, South Carolina, has been conducting an experiment in generosity toward restaurant servers for the past year or so. They have been tipping generously in restaurants around the city. When they tip they leave a card that reads, "It's time for some change!" They have flooded

> the city with these cards. They are reshaping the way Charlestonians see tipping and generosity.

Generosity Generator: *Build an abundance mentality.*

If you have a deprivation mentality, you can't give. You can't afford to give because you won't have enough for yourself, or so you think. It may be that you just need to redefine what you can afford. A rich person isn't one who has the most stuff; a rich person is one who can live with the least.

> *"If you are lonely, I will call...*
> *I love you*
> *I am the milkman of human kindness.*
> *I will leave an extra pint."* [2]
> —Billy Bragg, British Punk Rock Pioneer

Generosity Generator: *Give what you need.*

We needed money to buy a piece of land. We had some of the money, but not nearly enough to make the down payment. The Christmas season was approaching, so we also needed a significant amount of cash for a huge, free gift-wrapping project we had planned for the days before Christmas at a local mall.

However, we learned of another church that was also building a facility. We challenged people in our church to give to that church *before* they began to give to our church's property fund. With just a few days' notice, our church gave a surprise check for about thirty-five thousand dollars to the other church. By the following summer, we not only paid our down payment but were able to burn the mortgage at our annual church picnic.

Generosity Generator:
Give what you don't have, and God will give what you could never produce for yourself.

God is in the business of multiplying back to us what we offer to him. Make your resources available and God will repay you in ways that you can't imagine.

> *If you want to cut down on the number of relatives hanging around, borrow money from the rich ones and lend money to the ones who are poor. You'll never see any of them again.*
> —The Prairie Rambler

> *Best recipe for a prize-winning "sponge" cake: Borrow the butter, borrow the eggs, borrow the milk, and ask a neighbor if she will bake it in her oven.*

Generosity Generator:
Take a risk when you can't see the way forward.

Even when you can't see the specific outcome, pray for courage, perseverance, and a risk-taking attitude. The rewards for those who risk are great and far worth stepping out for.

> **GIVE IT AWAY!**
> A big money gift is weighing heavily on members of a small church. St. Mary's United Methodist Church in St. Mary's, Washington, received a gift of

$60 million, enough to pay its annual budget for the next 210 years, according to news reports. Warren Bailey, who attended the church as a child, left the money when he died at age 88.

Parishioners and church leaders are at a loss for what to do with it.

How to Increase the Level of Generosity at Your Church

- Every once in a while—maybe on Mother's Day—take up an offering and give it away to another church or ministry that is in need. Great plans are carried out by great churches.
- Tap into people's unique desires to give. If you only provide one way for people to give, you are limiting people's giving opportunities. Have different projects people can give to, ways you can pull on their heartstrings. For example, requested year-end giving probably ought not to be for the facility fund but for something for the poor that will have a natural appeal.

ENDNOTES

1. Jack McConnell, MD, "And What Did You Do For Someone Today?" Newsweek (June 18, 2001), 12.
2. Billy Bragg, "The Milkman of Human Kindness," by Billy Bragg (London: Chappell Music Ltd., 1983).

Path 11: TRUE

The two of us were having dinner at a Southern California restaurant and were kidding around. At least, I thought this pastor of a prominent church was kidding. In fact, I had just taken a sip of tea and I nearly spit it out I was laughing so hard. But he wasn't laughing.

The words hung in the air: "I could never have fellowship with you because you don't hold to the same view of the end times as I do. That's too bad, because I like you as a friend."

He didn't know it, but at that point, I actually did hold to the same end-times viewpoint that he did. But I was so grieved by his attitude of hairsplitting what I saw as miniscule issues that I didn't have the heart to tell him that we actually agreed.

Even though he was my friend, I felt as if I were talking to a Pharisee. I agreed with this pastor's theological perspective, but he was willing to write me off because I violated his religious tradition.

Essentials, Traditions, Opinions

I've been doing some thinking since that time. I've been thinking about what's important and what's not that important. As I see it, there are levels of issues. The first layer is absolutely vital. I call this the *essentials*. Without agreement on these matters, we actually aren't even believers aligned with the church and its past two thousand years of history.

Beyond the essentials are *traditions*. Traditions, or denominational "distinctives," are what make the body of Christ rich and interesting. These traditions make it a diverse body instead of a single-celled ameba. All of us are a part of some sort of faith tradition. Some might think their church is completely nontraditional, but even in that nontraditionalness, a tradition has been established. These are the distinctives that are true for your group, things that make your group unique from other groups. They don't make you right, they make you different. Southern Baptists aren't better than United Methodists, but the two groups are distinct, theologically and socially. Most importantly, both of them are orthodox. They believe in the essentials and are therefore true followers of the Jesus of the Bible.

I am a part of the Vineyard movement. It is unique in several ways—perhaps most significantly in its worship and its approach to outreach. I have many Methodist and Baptist friends who would feel they were being tortured if they were forced to sit through a Vineyard service and miss their traditional hymns for a Sunday. That doesn't make one style right and another wrong. It makes each different and unique. Having been a Christian for more than twenty years, I've been exposed to a vast diversity of styles of worship. I don't understand all of them, but I appreciate all of them because they are nurturing various parts of the Church.

Last, there are *opinions*. The essentials form a very small circle since there are just a few things that we must believe to be authentic Christians.

The traditions from a significantly larger circle; we have more traditions that have developed over the years. But by far the largest circle is formed by our opinions. The longer we spend in the Christian life, the more we accumulate opinions. Some of our opinion-gathering is helpful. But we've all come to plenty of opinions that aren't all that helpful to us or anyone else. Unfortunately, we often hold to those opinions fiercely.

Examples of topics where opinions cluster are liberation theology, ecology, nuclear power, gun control, eschatology, and the role of women in ministry.

I have hundreds of opinions that I choose to not make part of my tradition nor part of my list of essentials. I typically don't bring these opinions up when I teach or preach. No doubt if you and I were to sit down over a cup of coffee and talk long enough about our various opinions, we would eventually come to a place of disagreement. These are issues we've both thought through for a long time, and we each have good reason to hold those opinions. But that doesn't keep us from being Christians on the same mission.

My church has about thirty pastors. We don't see eye to eye on all theological issues when it comes to the opinions category. That's OK, because we are close enough on the important issues.

> ***It is important to keep these circles in mind: a small one that is vital; a larger one that is negotiable; a vast one that is worth chatting about over a cup of coffee sometime.***

Fighting between brothers and sisters in the church is perpetuated when they forget the order of the circles. It happens when I make tradition essential instead of negotiable. Or, worse yet, it happens when I consider my opinion about a topic to be an essential. These dyslexic episodes must grieve the heart of God. When he has vital work for the church to be about, we have sometimes been found arguing about absolutely nonvital matters.

What Is Essential?

WHO JESUS IS

Perhaps there is really just one essential question. If we are talking about the same Jesus, the Jesus as revealed in the Scriptures, then we are on common ground and are brothers. Jesus is the beginning, the middle, and end of all discussions about orthodoxy.

Have you have ever spoken with people in cult groups who are trying to pass themselves off as Christian? Or have you talked about beliefs with conservative evangelicals, such as Mormons, who will readily say that they believe in Jesus as the son of God. They'll say that they believe that he is the way, the truth, and the life and that no one gets to the father but by him—but there's a catch. They're not talking about the unique Son of God—the one of a kind, capital S Son of God who was fully God and fully man at the same time. They aren't even talking about the same Father for that matter. Like members of cults, conservative evangelicals seek to explain away all the mystery of God with manmade analogies. Christians hold the essential belief that separates us from all of the cults: namely, that Jesus is God in the flesh. What's essential is that people are worshipping Jesus Christ as he is revealed in the Bible.

For a good study on the biblical Christ versus some of the imposter Christs commonly posed by the cults, I suggest *Kingdom of the Cults* by Walter Martin. He goes into great depth regarding the orthodox view of the Trinity and the Godhead. This is a great book to add to your library.

WHERE WE GET OUR TRUTH

We confine our search for truth to the pages of Scripture. Like Luther's, our conscience is held captive to the pages of the Bible. They are our guide to all moral questions. The Scripture is our source for inspired wisdom in life. It reveals the knowledge of God to us. It is the revelation of God's character and nature. Without it we would have no clear light or knowledge of God in this world.

There is tremendous spiritual confusion in our current culture. Many don't know their left hand from their right, spiritually speaking. An ad that promotes Deepak Chopra's latest book, *How to Know God*, says, "You don't have to believe in God to experience God."

HOW WE GET RIGHT WITH GOD

It is essential that we see we are lost in our sins because of our connection to our ancestors Adam and Eve. We are part of a lost race: the human race. We were born into sin and separated from God at birth. Before coming to Christ, all of us were spiritually blind and incapable of finding our way to God on our own. God, in his mercy and grace, made himself known to each of us in numerous ways by the working of the Holy Spirit in our lives. In short, he opens our eyes to our need for salvation.

We must repent, turn our lives over to the control of Christ, and put our futures in his hands. We must believe that his death on the cross was on our behalf. When we ask God to apply upon our lives the sacrificial blood of Jesus that was shed for us on the cross, we are, at that moment, made right with God. Our deep, inner, spiritual hunger is quenched only when we finally relinquish control of our lives to Jesus. In so giving our lives over to him, we, for the first time, experience the peace of God that surpasses understanding. It is that peace that we were designed to walk in.

Some see this entire action as a covenant that we enter during childhood, while others (myself included) view this as a process that takes place in each person's heart at some point after they reach an age of accountability. As long as each person has repented and placed his or her faith in Christ, we are in the same boat.

Dear Ann Landers: Remember "Smokeless Hoosier," who ate 120 candy canes in three weeks to quit his 40-year, five-pack-a-day smoking habit? You said he was ruining his teeth. By my calculations, this guy smoked 1,460,000 cigarettes in his lifetime—and you're concerned about his teeth? False teeth never killed anyone that I know of.

Simi Valley, Calif.

> Dear Simi: I agree, better to lose your teeth than your life, but even better to lose neither.
>
> *Permission granted by Ann Landers and Creators Syndicate.*

What Is Tradition?

In my observations, all growing, thriving churches are low on the scale of the tradition they come out of. You've probably heard of "Low Catholic." That means the church conducts mass in English, guitars replace the pipe organ, and the priest speaks in understandable and user-friendly language.

There is a low version of church in every denomination. For example, I describe my church as being "Low Vineyard." By definition, there are also "High Vineyard" churches where services are quite different from what we are doing in north Cincinnati. By "Low Vineyard," I mean that we worship for just twenty minutes. We have a quick and efficient couple of "plugs" (we don't have announcements). Our message is thirty minutes at the most, and we are done in sixty minutes total. We're pretty efficient. In and out—no one gets hurt.

In virtually every denomination, the high version is not growing. No one is looking for a tradition to join. People are looking for life, honesty, and authenticity. The high versions of church, no matter what their flavor, just don't sell to our postmodern culture that places such a high value on "realness." As one pastor friend of mine says of his own denomination:

> *"Some assembly of God may be required."*

What Are Opinions?

In my years of doing servant evangelism projects, I have had many conversations with not-yet-Christians who were trying to figure out the

Christian faith. The questions they ask tend to be very similar. Conversations often go something like this:

"There are so many versions of the Bible. I wouldn't know which one to pick up even if I were to begin to read it."

"You want to read a big, black Bible."

"There's so much in the Bible that I find confusing and contradictory. I just don't know."

"Which part don't you understand?"

"All of it."

"But what part have you read that gives you trouble?"

"Well, I actually haven't read any of it."

"Why don't you begin to read at the book of John, and we'll talk through the parts that you don't understand."

Another conversation I've had several times recently is a reflection of our times:

"You know the Bible? Well, I think, like, people didn't write it. But, like, a long time ago, aliens brought the Bible here and dropped it off on earth as a book to, like, help us learn how to get along with each other. That's what I think."

"Well, if that's true, like, don't you think that, if aliens went to all that trouble to come across the universe, you ought to at least read it?"

Usually they say, *"Well, like, yes."*

How to Become More True

Ask yourself the following questions:

- Are your *essentials* the same as those laid out in this chapter?
- What does your list of *traditions* look like?
- Are your *opinions* out of control?

PATHS TO THE PERFECTLY IMPERFECT CHURCH

Path 12: COOPERATIVE

As the woman worked in her garden, her not-yet-Christian neighbor approached her. He asked, "Are you a member of the big church?"

Earlier that day the woman had been a part of a citywide event in her hometown of Abbotsford, British Columbia, near Vancouver in western Canada. Christians in this city of about one hundred thousand began an experiment a couple of years ago. They banded together to serve their city in large-scale, creative, and profound ways. I have been privileged to be a part of training those doing outreach. It is always exciting to train motivated people.

At the last event they held, which they dubbed Love Abbotsford, some fourteen hundred people from thirty local churches came out for various serving projects around the city. Everyone wore a white T-shirt with a large heart on it and handed out cards to explain the projects. The cards didn't promote individual churches but the "big C" church in the city. The cards named the Love Abbotsford event and referred people to a shared Web site that explained the entire project. The day went smoothly. Many thousands of people were touched, and the participants came back enthused.

Now back to the woman working in her garden that afternoon. Her not-yet-Christian neighbor stopped by and asked, "Say, I was in town today and saw all the folks with T-shirts. Are you a part of the big church with the T-shirts?"

She thought for a second about her church, which had several hundred people. "Well, my church is pretty big."

The neighbor said, "No, the *really* big church, the one with the hundreds of people who were out on the town today—*that* church." She got it. Her heart was touched, she teared up, and she said, "*Yes, in fact, I am a part of the big church!*"

God is busy building the big church these days. If we are going to be a Perfectly Imperfect Church, we need to be larger than a single church. God has much for us to accomplish. We'll reach our potential only as we team up with the larger church.

I've been doing some dreaming. Dream with me for a bit.

What if...we realized the truth that we can't reach our city by ourselves, even if our church is large and well-equipped? We need an army made up of all the churches in our city.

What if...we were willing to cooperate with other churches, even churches that don't necessarily hold all the same traditions and opinions that we do?

What if...we prayed each weekend that God would bless the churches of the city first before he blessed our church—and we meant it? A good start would be something like this: "God, bless your church in this city with your presence in a significant way. And once you've blessed the other churches who love you, then come and bless us with your presence, as well."

What if...we really got along? The unchurched have no idea why we can't get along. People who don't go to church are extremely put off by churches that are in competition with one another. At a recent food give-away, a fellow stepped into our ministry bus and said, "I can't believe it!"

We said, "What, sir? We're just giving away food."

"I just can't believe it," he continued.

"What is it that you can't believe?"

"I've been on your church bus four times, and I haven't seen your church name anywhere on it—I can't believe it!"

There's a hunger in the unchurched world to see the church do altruistic things, and there's a double hunger for the same in the membership of the church.

What if...we looked out for one another in the church scene? If one church gets a good name, we will all benefit from it; if one church gets a bad name, we will all suffer for it. It only makes sense that we begin to take seriously the reputation of the entire church in the city.

What if...God doesn't see us as being in different churches? What if God just sees those people who don't belong to his church. It doesn't make sense to compete with other churches. Rather we need to seek the people who are not connected with any church. There are thousands of those folks nearby you.

What if...we came alongside other people's dreams and blessed those dreams? When we include other people, we join ourselves to their dreams. In most churches, the idea of "coming alongside someone" is an unwelcome idea—it sounds intrusive. That isn't what I'm talking about. I'm talking about the sorts of things that make everybody happy.

What if...we saw our well-being interwoven with the well-being of other churches in the city? We have a city-reaching perspective that requires the help of the entire church if we are to succeed. We will never accomplish much if our goal is to stop at the boundaries of our churches. For example, why not take offerings for other churches as the need presents itself. Churches that take offerings for other churches are churches with a great destiny. That sort of behavior is rare, but it would be great if churches became self-actualized enough to think beyond themselves.

What if...we lived out the truth that it really is better to give than to receive?

Some months ago in Cincinnati, fifty churches gathered together to reach out to a large portion of the city in a single day. After much planning and dreaming, we combined efforts to reach out and touch more than one hundred thousand people that day. Instead of promoting one church over another, all the churches used the same connection card. The card simply explained that the project was something that showed God's love in a practical way and referenced "ServeCincinnati.com" as the sponsor of the act of kindness. Billboards throughout the city advertised that simple Web site address with a hand engraved heart. (Check out the permanent Web site at ServeCincinnati.com for more on the project.) Outreaches were going on throughout the city; the largest one was giving away one hundred thousand soft drinks (one thousand each at one hundred locations around the city). We also held car washes and painted doors in run-down neighborhoods. All of the outreaches were done in just three to four hours. A beautiful, rare unity was achieved.

When it was finished, the words of Ronald Reagan came to mind—"When no one cares who gets the credit, there's a lot of good that can get done."

"Are You From the Big Church?"

I hope so, for that is the future. Active membership in the big church is what the Holy Spirit wants for the church today.

Path 13: LEADING OUT

Draw, Antonio, and do not waste time.
—Michelangelo

No one had started a new church in Chillocothe (CHILL-o-caw-thee) in decades. This medium-sized town in central Ohio just wasn't on many church planters' most-admired-cities list. Just the same, my friend Steve Goode felt called to launch a new church there. But how do you start something in a town that has zero church-planting momentum? How do you get going when no one is inviting you to come?

Steve launched out in a small way: He and his wife gave away coffee at the local high school football games. They were there game after game on cold evenings to help people ward off the chill. It wasn't too long before a couple of curious individuals asked Steve what in the world he was doing at these cold games every Friday night. Soon these strangers became friends and joined him in his outreach. With a handful of people, he had a glimmer of momentum. Those people joined his first home group. The plan was simple: to meet in small groups to learn to love one another and then to do an excellent job of reaching out into the community in practical ways.

That was four years ago, and the small group of coffee distributors has mushroomed to more than three hundred people each weekend. They are still going out into the community each week doing a variety of outward-focused projects. The church is a Perfectly Imperfect Church by all accounts. That's what I call outward-facing leadership.

Where Are You Facing?

All leaders are aimed in some direction. The question is, are they aimed inward or outward? It's a matter of healthy or unhealthy, growing or not growing, moving forward or stagnating.

If I find someone who is an expert at building disciples, I make it a priority to have that person *do* things with people, not just *teach* people new things. Being a disciple isn't primarily about going to church, praying, and reading the Bible. Being a disciple means doing the deeds that Jesus did.

We don't expect our people to feel a certain something or express a certain emotion but to develop certain behaviors. Even if I am in a bad mood, I can still rake a leaf or wash a car. In the first two years of discipleship—both for individuals and for new churches—we establish the rudiments of doing rather than just talking. Once that's established in our hearts, we will do it and teach our friends about it.

We need to be the sort of people who lead outward continually. Scripture calls us to lead out: "Therefore go and make disciples" (Matthew 28:19). We live in the age of "Go," according to the calling of God upon the church. If we are to obey, we can only be the church that leads out instead of in.

We can lead out in a number of ways.

LEAD OUT...BY BEING DECISIVE.

Right now, more than at any other time, the church needs leaders who know where they are going. We don't need to make rash decisions; we simply need to make decisions that are carefully considered and—once seen clearly—courageously acted upon. Courage is a commodity that leadership circles always need more of.

TAKE A CHANCE

Did I ever tell you about the young Zode,
Who came to two signs at the fork of the road?
One said, "To Place One," and the other, "Place Two."
So the Zode had to make up his mind what to do.
Well...the Zode scratched his head. And his chin. And his pants.
And he said to himself, "I'll be taking a chance.
If I go to Place One, now that place may be hot!
So how do I know if I'll like it or not?
On the other hand, though I'll sort of be a fool,
If I go to Place Two, I might find it too cool.
In that case, I may catch a chill and turn blue!
On the other hand, though, if Place One is too high,
I may catch a terrible earache and die!
So Place Two may be the best!
On the other hand, though...
What might happen to me if Place Two is too low?
I might get some strange pain in my toe!"
Then he said, "On the other hand, though...
On the other hand, though...On the other hand, though..."
And for thirty-six and one-half hours, that poor Zode
Made starts and stops at the fork in the road,
Saying, "Don't take a chance, you may not be right."

> Then he got an idea that was wonderfully bright!
> "Play safe!" cried the Zode. "I'll play safe! I'm no dunce!
> I'll simply start off for both places at once!"
> And that's how the Zode, who would not take a chance,
> Got no place at all, with a split in his pants.
> *—author unknown*

LEAD OUT...BY TAKING BOLD RISKS.

How does your leadership team deal with failure? Think of the way embarrassment and understanding come together when a "mistake" is made.

What's most typical is *high embarrassment* accompanied with *low understanding*. The church is known for shaming and blaming when mistakes are made. What if we inverted that arrangement so that when things went wrong people experienced *low embarrassment* accompanied with *high understanding?* How much further ahead would we be if, when things went wrong, they weren't viewed as errors as much as they were seen as learning experiences that propel us forward?

I am best known for the large church that I planted some years ago on the north side of Cincinnati. I've also been pretty successful at helping other people start churches. But what many people don't know is that I still regularly fail at church planting. Every year I step out to coach the planting of a number of new churches. Every year some make it and some don't. I always start out thinking that every new church will make it and excel. I'm always somewhat surprised and very disappointed when a church doesn't make it.

LEAD OUT...BY TAKING THE LEAD YOURSELF.

Ernest Shackleton was the leader of the crew of the HMS Endurance. The ship, a British scientific exploratory vessel, set sail from London just prior to the sudden beginning of World War I. When the ship became icebound near the South Pole, no one was able to come to the crew's aid.

Finally it became apparent that no one was going to rescue them, and Ernest Shackleton changed his goal from traversing the antarctic continent to saving the lives of his crew.

Eventually the ice crushed the ship; the crew was stuck with mere tents and several lifeboats. Ultimately they decided to send six men to try to reach a whaling station eight hundred miles away. Shackleton led the way, and the rescue party shoved off. Their venture was a huge gamble; the men had only a sextant and a hand compass to guide them across the most dangerous ocean in the world.

After seventeen days at sea, they made it to the island, but steep mountains and uncharted territory lay between them and rescue. Leaving three men in the cove with the boat. Shackleton led the other two men into the mountains, headed "magnetic East" toward a whaling station—they hoped. For thirty-six hours straight, the men climbed and slid. At one point, the way forward required jumping into a waterfall. Finally the party of three arrived at the whaling station. After a couple of days of recuperation, Shackleton led a rescue team back to the icebound crew. Not a single man of the Endurance crew was lost.

I have read a number of books about the voyage of the Endurance, and they all point to Shackleton's incredible activist leadership as the key to everyone's survival. [1]

> ***"His outstanding characteristics were his care of, and anxiety for, the lives and well-being of all his men."***
> —Frank Worsley of Ernest Shackleton

Shackleton's outstanding quality was his penchant for being a leader who did what he talked about. He didn't direct a rescue plan from the sidelines. He got into the middle of things. He took risks along with his men. The crew respected him for it and drew strength from his willingness to go forward regardless of fears he might have had. Shackleton's lead-by-doing approach was the key to the crew's survival against all odds in the harshest imaginable of environments.

LEAD OUT...BY TEACHING YOUR PEOPLE TO BE PRACTICAL-DOERS, NOT STUDENT-MYSTICS.

A dichotomy exists in the church between theoretical and action-oriented Christianity. As you might guess, I am a big advocate of the practical, action side of things. I don't see great value in increasing our list of theories. It seems to me that, if we would simply apply the lengthy list of topics that we have all learned over the past several years and stay away from more theory, we would probably grow as a result.

The student-mystic role is what many new followers of Christ are encouraged to achieve. However, that model of discipleship doesn't work and serves only to alienate new believers from their old friends. A much better approach is to have new followers make a commitment to spend time with the poor. The poor are our old friends who are looking for Christ. We are the bridge between them and the One they need to know.

LEAD OUT...BY FOCUSING BEYOND OURSELVES.

Leadership is based on action, on doing, on serving. The Greek root word for *deacon* suggests a "dust kicker," or someone who is so busy doing the work of ministry that he or she kicks up a cloud of dust with a flurry of serving.

Outward Focused People

We are going for it for life is short.

The day after the September 11 bombing of the World Trade Center buildings our entire staff of over 100 piled into two busses and went to downtown Cincinnati's highest point, the top of the Carew Tower. There we prayed for our nation and our city for an extended time. As we prayed individually, I found myself asking God to make our lives count. With the fresh shock of September 11 in my mind, I couldn't help but think that life is short and unpredictable.

If what we are calling "ministry" isn't generating changed lives, then we need to seriously examine how much time we are spending in planning versus doing.

Leading Destiny

Let's lead out and develop some perfectly imperfect churches that are committed to being what God wants them to be in this broken and needy world.

ENDNOTE

1. Caroline Alexander, *The Endurance* (New York: Alfred A. Knopf, 1999).

Group Publishing, Inc.
Attention: Product Development
P.O. Box 481
Loveland, CO 80539
Fax: (970) 679-4370

Evaluation for
The Perfectly Imperfect Church

Please help Group Publishing, Inc. continue to provide innovative and useful resources for ministry. Please take a moment to fill out this evaluation and mail or fax it to us. Thanks!

• • •

1. As a whole, this book has been (circle one)

not very helpful — very helpful

1 2 3 4 5 6 7 8 9 10

2. The best things about this book:

3. Ways this book could be improved:

4. Things I will change because of this book:

5. Other books I'd like to see Group publish in the future:

6. Would you be interested in field-testing future Group products and giving us your feedback? If so, please fill in the information below:

Name ______________________________

Church Name ______________________________

Denomination ____________________ Church Size ______________

Church Address ______________________________

City ____________________ State __________ ZIP __________

Church Phone ______________________________

E-mail ______________________________